Statistics
for Kids

Statistics for Kids

Model-Eliciting Activities to Investigate Concepts in Statistics

Scott A. Chamberlin, Ph.D.

Routledge
Taylor & Francis Group

NEW YORK AND LONDON

First published in 2013 by Prufrock Press Inc.

Published in 2021 by Routledge
605 Third Avenue, New York, NY 10017
2 Park Square, Milton Park, Abingdon, Oxon OX14 4RN

Routledge is an imprint of the Taylor & Francis Group, an informa business

Copyright © 2013 Taylor & Francis Group

Production design by Raquel Trevino

ISBN: 9781032142135 (hbk)
ISBN: 9781618210227 (pbk)

DOI: 10.4324/9781003238201

Table of Contents

Introduction

This book is unlike any other book on the market, for several reasons. First, books are rarely written for use solely in statistics. Second, statistics books are infrequently written for students of advanced intellect in grades 4–6. Third, until recently, mathematical modeling activities were used almost exclusively with undergraduate and graduate students at the college level.

In the introduction, readers will learn how the chapters are organized and what information can be found in each, important definitions, why the book pertains to statistics but not probability, the method used for selecting the topics, why model-eliciting activities (MEAs) are used to facilitate consideration of topics in statistics, the learning theory used, and some general information for using MEAs.

Arrangement of Each Chapter

With a focus on helping teachers, curriculum coordinators, instructional facilitators, mathematics club directors, summer program teachers, and others implement the activities highlighted in this book, each chapter is comprised of:
- a background to the activity,
- the subject focus of the chapter,
- the activity itself,
- links to National Council of Teachers of Mathematics (NCTM) content standards,
- potential student responses,

DOI: 10.4324/9781003238201-1

- questions to pose to students as the activity is being implemented, and
- implementation techniques including time required, presentation formats, and other helpful tips.

The Principles and Standards for School Mathematics (PSSM; NCTM, 2000) have been used for this book even though, at the time of print, nearly all of the states have adopted the Common Core State Standards for Mathematics (Common Core State Standards Initiative, 2010). The PSSM has been used for several reasons; most notably, all states adhere to it in some capacity, and it has greatly affected the development of the Common Core State Standards. In addition, the creators of the PSSM appear to have invested far greater effort in paying attention to statistics and probability than the creators of the Common Core State Standards have, particularly in grades 4–6. Further, in general the correlation between the Common Core State Standards and the PSSM appears to be somewhat strong. Finally, it is important to note that specific standards have not been mentioned. Instead, expectations (i.e., more specific tasks that NCTM deems necessary for students to learn) are discussed to help teachers realize what mathematical concepts these MEA tasks will cover.

Content Focus of Individual Chapters

In each chapter, readers will be provided with one activity (MEA) that demands investigation and the creation of a mathematical model to describe phenomena in statistics. The emphases for respective chapters are:
- Chapter 1: trends,
- Chapter 2: spread of data,
- Chapter 3: measures of central tendency,
- Chapter 4: variability,
- Chapter 5: correlation,
- Chapter 6: covariation, and
- Chapter 7: statistical sampling.

It is important to note that each chapter has a focus, but, due to the open-ended nature of MEAs, it cannot be guaranteed that the focus of the chapter will be the only concept explored by students. As an example, the focus of Chapter 1 is on trends; however, students may stray into other concepts because using various representations of data can help students solidify mathematical models.

Definitions Used in the Book

Readers must understand several definitions in the book to successfully implement the activities. To start, *model-eliciting activities* are simply activities that demand the creation of a mathematical model to solve a given problem. A typical follow-up question is: "What constitutes a mathematical model?" This is an oft-posed question and, depending on the source, one can find radically different answers. In short, for MEAs, a mathematical model is any explanation, often connoted by symbolic or other forms of representation, which is generalizable to future, similar situations. For example, a formula is closely related to a mathematical model. To compute the area (A) of a circle, one uses the formula $A = \pi r^2$ because one multiplies the relationship between the circumference of the circle relative to the diameter of the same circle (π) by the radius (r) squared. This is a proven method that Archimedes derived almost 2,300 years ago and it is an explanation that can be used repeatedly to compute the area of a circle. From a statistical perspective, a mathematical model is created when "a mathematical system is interpreted in terms of real objects or events" (Hays, 1994, p. 3).

The definition of *statistics* is also of interest. As was the case with mathematical models, statistics has many definitions. NCTM (2000) has replaced the word statistics with the term *data analysis*. This may be selling statistics short insofar as it implies that statistics is merely comprised of the analysis of data. Statisticians have a much broader interest in the entire process than simply analyzing data. In fact, statisticians actually create protocols for research, design instruments to collect data, sample populations, collect data, analyze data, interpret data, and draw conclusions from data. The recurring theme in this field, of course, is data. Without data, no analysis can be done and statistical procedures cannot be used. As such, all MEAs in this book are data-based.

A final definition of interest to readers is the somewhat nebulous conception of *giftedness*. As Gross (2000) suggested, there are many levels of giftedness. This book has been written to serve mildly to profoundly gifted students, with an emphasis on mildly to highly gifted students. This book is appropriate if a student has some mathematical capabilities beyond what typical students might have. MEAs can serve fairly disparate audiences: For example, a grade 6 student with grade 10 mathematical capabilities can be as similarly challenged as a grade 6 student with grade 7 capabilities, as illustrated by Chamberlin (2002). It is for this reason precisely that MEAs hold great promise for magnet, pull-out, and inclusion practices in gifted education. Simply stated, gifted students in mathematics will find challenge in doing MEAs.

Content Focus Is Statistics, Not Probability

Many will question how a book can be assembled in which statistics is discussed, but not probability. Technically, the two areas are often merged because it is difficult to discuss one without the other. To that end, some consideration of probability will undoubtedly arise as activities are implemented and solved by students. However, the principal emphasis in this book is on statistics. As previously stated, there are few books that deal with statistics in grades 4–6, fewer statistics books for gifted students in this grade band, and no books that use MEAs as the vehicle for promoting learning among such students. Couple all of this information with the notion that statistics is likely the most neglected of all content areas in mathematics, yet it is arguably the most applicable to real-life situations, and a disaster is at hand. If we don't prepare our students to engage in statistical reasoning, they will be unprepared when they encounter situations in which statistical demands exist. Statistics have tremendous real-world importance; Hays (1994), for example, referred to statistics as "how things are" (p. 3).

The Selection of Topics

Invariably, whenever one writes a book on selected topics, readers pose the logical question, "So, how did you (the author) decide on topics?" This is a valid question. The concepts were not selected randomly. Instead, a systematic approach was used to ascertain which topics are of paramount importance in the development of statistical reasoning at young ages (10–12).

Several parties were solicited to identify seminal topics. First, experts in statistics were personally contacted. Second, national and international reports and publications that detailed information on statistics were used. With respect to individuals of prominence, Drs. David Moore and George McCabe at Purdue University were initially contacted. Their recommendation was to investigate the American Statistical Association website to gain clarity on K–12 statistics concepts (http://amstat.org/education/index.cfm) and to contact Joan Garfield at the University of Minnesota. Drs. McCabe and Moore are considered by many to be the leading experts in the world on statistics, but they work mostly with undergraduate- and graduate-level statistics students and research. Dr. Joan Garfield is considered by many to be the leading expert in K–12 statistics in the world. Following repeated correspondence with Dr.

Garfield, a list was provided that matched quite closely with the author's initial list and with concepts identified in many reports.

Regarding reports, the *Guidelines for Assessment and Instruction in Statistics Education* (*GAISE*) *Report* published by the American Statistical Association (n.d.) meshed nicely with the list compiled by Dr. Garfield and the author. Subsequently, syllabi and any information available on Advanced Placement (AP) Statistics courses were utilized. In addition, the concepts promoted in the *Principles and Standards for School Mathematics* (NCTM, 2000) content standards were used along with Dr. Garfield's book entitled *Developing Students' Statistical Reasoning* (Garfield & Ben-Zvi, 2008). Finally, the author's expertise was considered given his familiarity with statistics courses at the graduate level and a deep understanding of mathematics and gifted education.

Model-Eliciting Activities as a Curricular Tool

MEAs have a relatively short history in education—approximately 35 years—but they have had a rather profound impact on student learning in mathematics (Lesh, Hoover, Hole, Kelly, & Post, 2000). As the title indicates, MEAs are problem-solving tasks created by mathematics educators to encourage students to investigate concepts in mathematics through the creation of mathematical models. Initially, MEAs were created to investigate how students thought in mathematical situations. In the early to mid-1970s, researchers wanted a comprehensive and systematic method of gathering data about the processes students utilize to solve mathematics problems (Resnick & Ford, 1981). At the time, these activities were referred to as *thought-revealing activities* or *case studies for kids*. Several years later, these tasks took on their own identity when Dr. Richard Lesh referred to them as *model-eliciting activities* and several researchers made the realization that such activities have great potential to challenge students mathematically. The inception of MEAs in mathematics classrooms arose simultaneous to the emphasis on conceptual learning.

Each MEA has six principles that must be met prior to it being deemed complete (Lesh et al., 2000). These characteristics provide uniformity in the tasks and they ensure that learning demands are consistent from task to task. The six design principles are: the model construction principle, the reality principle, the self-assessment principle, the construct documentation principle, the construct shareability and reusability principle, and the effective prototype principle (Chamberlin & Moon, 2005; Lesh et al., 2000). These principles speak of the applicability of the models and the link to real-life settings. As a result, they further substantiate the utilitarian nature of mathematics. Those who are interested can find more information about these six principles in Appendix A at the back of this book.

Model-eliciting activities also foster the investigation of concepts through a group approach (Dark, 2003). In being consistent with the real-world nature of MEAs, it seems unrealistic that vocational demands of workers today are such that any one individual will work on a project exclusively alone. More often than not, it seems to be natural that individuals work on a project in a team setting. It is therefore suggested that students work in groups of three to complete each MEA.

Learning Theories Employed

The theory behind the book is that students will have the opportunity to create mathematical models that can be more formally investigated with algorithms in subsequent months or years. For example, students may not officially quantify a correlation coefficient in the stock market problem, but they can perhaps create a graph and/or line of best fit that may ultimately help them create a mathematical model and gain deeper conceptual understanding of a correlation (which is nothing more than a relationship that has been quantified). In the future, when the formal notation, symbolic representation, and algorithms are explained, it is likely that students will be able to make sense of the statistical concepts in the investigation (Hiebert et al., 1997). No specific learning theory is endorsed in this book, as multiple learning theories have influenced the author and peer authors of MEAs.

Implementing MEAs

MEAs are different than any other type of mathematical problem-solving task for various structural reasons. In most situations, mathematical problems are posed to solvers after a procedure has been revealed to solve the problem. As Hiebert et al. (1997) stated, this is not *problematic* for students. For instance, if the algorithm for how to compute an arithmetic mean is shown and discussed in class and then students are asked to compute 10 arithmetic means in a problem or on a worksheet, the sense of novelty has been removed from the problem. The problem is therefore not "problematic." On the other hand, MEAs are problematic for students because they are asked to solve problems for which the answer is not known a priori (or prior to it being given). Moreover, a solution path is not revealed prior to solving the problem. Students typically have sufficient mathematical knowledge to solve the problem, but they need to access the information.

When MEAs are implemented, instructors should follow several steps. First, a handout providing background information is often assigned the night before the problem is implemented. This is a task that students are quite capable of doing on their own prior to implementation of the problem. After reading the initial handout, students can then work on the readiness or warm-up questions the night before actual problem solving occurs. These questions provide a basic check for comprehension and are intended to generate interest in and engagement with the activity. As class begins, the instructor can pose the readiness questions to the entire class and create a context for talking about the forthcoming problem. The next step is to review the problem statement and any data tables included with the problem. Once the problem statement has been clarified with all groups of students, the groups can then start to work on the task. At the conclusion of the problem-solving process, groups should be asked to discuss respective solutions in front of the entire class.

Additional considerations for implementation exist. For instance, instructors should consider the social dynamics of groups and develop them to maximize learning during the problem-solving process. It is a generally agreed-upon principle by MEA implementers that groups of three appear to work most efficiently. When placing students in groups, the extent to which students get along with one another socially is a consideration. In addition, balancing strengths and weaknesses may also be a consideration. Fewer than three students in a group can create problems because one student can dominate the solution and more than three students in a group can be difficult because some students can become rather passive in the solution process. Materials should be carefully considered and offered to students. For most problems, a very elementary calculator, ample data tables, and paper and pencils or pens for making notes on the solution process and for manipulating data could be provided. An advanced calculator is not suggested for these activities because, surprisingly, it may be less efficient for rather elementary computations.

Students customarily engage in multiple iterations of a model in an effort to create the most sophisticated one. This is often referred to as "expressing, testing, and revising" (Lesh, Young, & Fenewald, 2009, p. 278). In short, it is quite unorthodox for students, or any problem solvers, to create the most sophisticated mathematical model on the first attempt. Just as engineers do when designing a product, students make slight changes to prototypes, which often result in a more refined model. This is the case with MEAs and this is yet another reason that these problems vary from typical mathematical problem-solving tasks. Instructors are advised to set up the problem, make sure students know what their responsibilities are in solving the problem, and then step back and let students work. Many teachers have set up the problem in such detail that the problematic nature of the task was removed. This defeats the purpose of doing the MEA and it thwarts painstaking efforts that the author has invested to create a solid MEA.

When doing the MEAs, if students are heading in the direction of an incomplete answer, the instructor should help them realize why the solution is incomplete. Although many of the most complete solutions to the problems in this book rely on advanced statistical knowledge and procedures, it is important to see how students address the various problems that arise when attempting to create a solution. Oftentimes, their ingenuity will lead them to address concerns in surprisingly satisfactory ways. However, if students are struggling to grasp a mathematical concept, instructors are well advised to let the students come to the misconception and to revisit the group to see that the misconception was clarified. If students do not identify the misconception, then the instructor will need to pose a question to help the group identify the shortcoming in its response.

At the conclusion of all MEAs, students should be capable of presenting their mathematical models (i.e., solutions) to the entire class. This may require a PowerPoint presentation, notes on a piece of paper for use with a document camera (or an overhead sheet), or an actual poster or other product detailing the solution. The presentations need to be in great enough detail that all students can implement the solution through the information offered in the presentation. During the presentation, the instructor must pay close attention to determine whether participants understand explained solutions. Questions may need to be posed for particularly ambiguous discussions. It has been the case in the past, often with gifted students, that a fairly sophisticated solution was compromised by an unclear presentation. Periodically, groups have mathematical discussions of great interest for their grade level, but they fail to communicate their processes carefully. The instructor should be ready to clarify points made by presenters that are simply unclear. In addition, instructors should pay close attention to various solution paths prior to presentations so that multiple presentations are not duplicated. This approach saves valuable instruction time, and it saves groups the embarrassment of reiterating information already discussed by other groups. A helpful tactic to illustrate that all groups' solutions are valued is to pose questions to groups after the presentations that call attention to the similarity of solutions. For example, if groups A, B, and C have nearly identical solutions and group A presents to the class, the instructor can ask groups B and C if they did anything differently from what was presented. This can also be helpful in the event that group A does not clearly explicate its solution and group B or C realizes the shortcoming in the presentation. By giving the nonpresenting groups the opportunity to add to the presentation, it can become a more comprehensive presentation than was otherwise given.

Most MEAs require between 45–60 minutes for completion. Groups should be largely done documenting their solution in 60 minutes. Presentations will require an additional class period and can range from 30–60 minutes contingent upon the number of groups in the class and the number of solutions. Instructors should be diligent in posing questions to groups as they present. Questions may be used to clarify ambiguous points and/or to highlight particularly insightful or creative solutions. In some instances, solutions may solidify misconceptions that many students have about the particular problem or a mathematical procedure recently discussed. As such, hastily concluding presentations is ill advised. Moreover, instructors should realize that as groups give increasingly more presentations, they will likely become more efficient and productive than they were in initial attempts. Although no set metric exists, it is advised that MEAs be done approximately every 3–5 weeks, though the frequency of implementation falls to the discretion of the facilitator.

Assessment Concerns

Many educators, when implementing MEAs, question the criteria that constitute poor, acceptable, and exemplary models. Due to the open-ended nature of these activities, there is no clear-cut line between "good" and "bad" responses. Potential solutions are discussed to give instructors an idea of the range of complexity they can expect of students' responses, and to point out strengths and weaknesses of these various solutions. Appendix B provides an example response to the problem presented in Chapter 1, and readers are advised to visit this section prior to implementing any model-eliciting activities in their classrooms.

Caveats

It is important to convey two caveats prior to reading this book. First, sample responses have been provided in each chapter. These solutions become progressively more sophisticated: Solution 2 is more sophisticated than Solution 1, and Solution 5 is more sophisticated than Solutions 1–4. Exceptionally bright students or those with previous statistics experience may correctly identify the most advanced solutions, but by no means should these responses be expected of each and every group, or even a majority of them.

Second, the chapters were specifically arranged so that topics get progressively more difficult from the start of the book to the finish. Hence, although success in one MEA is not contingent upon having completed the previous activity, the likelihood of success with any MEA may be predicated upon understanding the concepts presented in earlier chapters.

A critical component to fully utilizing the MEAs is the student-led and instructor-moderated discussion that takes place upon completion of the activity. Instructors should have several pieces of information prior to starting the discussions. First, instructors must be acquainted with all group-created mathematical models. Second, instructors should have two or three talking points prepared prior to the discussion. The instructor should highlight important details that are not fully elucidated or are altogether omitted by students, and can use this time to further clarify any mathematical procedures relevant to the solution that were not grasped or adequately understood. The amount of time necessary to invest in group-led discussions is contingent upon several factors such as diversity of mathematical models, the number of groups present, and the specificity of the content topics.

Resources for Implementing and Understanding MEAs

Several resources discussing implementation techniques for MEAs exist, both online an in print. The article "Model-Eliciting Activities: A Case-Based Approach for Getting Students Interested in Material Science and Engineering" by Tamara J. Moore and published in the *Journal of Materials Education* is one such resource (it can be accessed online at http://matdl.org/jme/files/2008/06/moore_jme_model_eliciting_activities.pdf). Others include the webpages Model Eliciting Activities and Reflecting Tools for Problem Solving (http://litre.ncsu.edu/sltoolkit/MEA/MEA.htm) and How to Teach with Model-Eliciting Activities (http://serc.carleton.edu/sp/library/mea/how.html). In addition, the Lesh, Galbraith, Haines, and Hurford (2009) publication provides a fairly theoretical approach to understanding mathematical modeling in general. Chapter 2 and 24 are particularly salient to model-eliciting activities. It may be helpful, however, to have some understanding of MEAs prior to reading these proceedings.

Emphasis on Technical Writing

It is imperative that instructors have the groups carefully document the processes used to design their mathematical models. Instructors should remember that one of the six principles for creating a mathematical model when doing MEAs is the construct documentation principle (Lesh et al., 2000). Moreover, the term *processes* is used in reference to the ways in which groups solved the problem because many times, only one process will be discussed in the presentation. For the sake of discussion, the various processes that did not work should be listed because discussing why they did not work can be as insightful as discussing processes that did work. Consequently, it is most important that groups accurately detail all attempts made at solving the problem.

One of the long-held concerns of MEA writers is that technical writing, the genre of writing used most often in mathematics and other STEM disciplines, is noticeably absent from elementary and middle grades instruction. MEAs offer teachers promising opportunities to engage students in technical writing responsibilities by carefully demanding that they document all steps used to solve a problem. One caveat is that when groups complete their first MEA, instructors may need to check their letter to the client to see that it is accurate. (The client is the person or group for whom the mathematical model is being produced.) Groups often omit steps in haste and the excitement of creating their first mathematical model may be a reason for skipped steps. Hence, it behooves instructors to perpetually remind students to have a piece of paper off to the side to document the various steps used to solve the problem. Students should be made to think of the process as akin to driving to a new location without assistance from a GPS or map. This helpful analogy can give students insight into the fact that not all problems are solved correctly the first time. When in new territory, repeated attempts may need to be made to ultimately find the actual location. If one is driving and misses a turn, it should be noted that the error was made. Similarly, if someone designs a method to replace standard deviation and the designed model is not an inadequate one, the process should be noted in the final letter to the client.

As groups write an increasingly greater number of MEA letters, they will likely become more and more specific and proficient in their technical writing skills. This is a positive byproduct of this interdisciplinary approach and it should be encouraged, as MEAs demand such skill. Often, neophyte MEA instructors wonder what sort of information should be included in the final letter or documentation. Lesh and colleagues (2000) mentioned that mathematical "kinds of systems (objects, relations, operations, patterns and regularities) that students were thinking with and about" (p. 628) should be the focus of explanations.

Expectations of Student Knowledge

It may seem somewhat counterintuitive that students undertaking highly sophisticated, complex activities need not have a great deal of background knowledge in statistics. Nevertheless, anecdotal data suggests that students with a strong conceptual understanding of number sense and operations are typically well prepared to experience success with statistics and model-eliciting activities. This is the case because number sense and operations is considered the basis or gateway for understanding other content areas of mathematics such as geometry, algebra, and statistics. Consequently, students with a deep conceptual understanding of mathematics in general will be capable of successfully completing all MEAs in this book. Previous experiences with the topics—trends, spread of data, measures of central tendency, variability, correlation, covariation, and statistical sampling—are not necessary and in many cases not desired because conceptions may interfere with students' ability to successfully create mathematical models.

Disclaimers

There are two disclaimers to this book. First, this book was specifically written so that students could do the problems without software. Later, software should be introduced if it has not been introduced already. However, completing these problems without software increases the likelihood that students will be provided with a strong conceptual understanding of statistics. In fact, after completing these problems, students in grades 4–6 may be ahead of many high school and some college students who have simply engaged in procedural learning of elementary statistical concepts. Subsequent to completing activities in this book, students should be introduced to software such as Microsoft Excel, R, SYSTAT, Stata, Minitab, Fathom, and SPSS. For very advanced students who may have a propensity for computer programming, SAS and other similar software products could be used.

Second, in the section of each chapter entitled Links to NCTM Content Standards, grade levels beyond 4–6 are used to align content expectations. This was done because the focus of the book is on serving the needs of students of advanced intellect in grades 4–6. This precipitates the question: "Is the focus of the book on acceleration or enrichment?" The answer is yes. With intellectually advanced mathematics students in grades 4–6, it is the belief of the author that acceleration and enrichment need not be mutually exclusive. Further, with the curricular approach used (i.e., model-eliciting activities), students can actively engage with material several grade levels beyond their age and still successfully make sense of statistical concepts (Hiebert et al., 1997).

Additional Information

Additional information regarding MEAs, the design principles behind them, the impact of affect in mathematics, and other statistics concerns can be found in Appendix A in the back of this book.

Chapter 1

Trends

The 10,000 Meters Problem

Track and field is a well-known sport in the United States. However, in the rest of the world, track and field events are referred to as Athletics, the larger category of sports to which they belong. (Henceforth, *Athletics* will refer to track and field and *athletics* to sports in general.) Athletics is considered by many to be the most international of all sports because people from every country in the world can participate in the events. Consequently, the top athletes in Athletics events come from a wide variety of countries.

For years, the three largest revenue-generating sports in the United States—baseball, football, and basketball—have been bestowed with endless statistics and statisticians to provide analysis of their games. Athletics also benefits from statistical analysis, particularly at the international level, and Athletics provides the context for this problem, designed to introduce the topic of trends. In this activity, students are asked to analyze data of 17 collegiate athletes and create a mathematical model to explain a trend in the data. Each MEA has a client (i.e., the person or group for whom the mathematical model is being produced). In this MEA, the client is Coach Mike Hall. Coach Hall needs to be more systematic in his recruiting efforts. Rather than just guessing at which athletes will develop rapidly, Coach Hall really wants to have athletes that can contribute greatly to his team and he feels that statistics may provide insight regarding which athletes to recruit most heavily. Moreover, the discovery of certain patterns (i.e., trends) might inspire Mike to change his distribution of scholarship money and award partial scholarships to more athletes rather than full scholarships to fewer athletes. For example, if athletes that have run a specified time (e.g., quicker than 32:30 for 10,000 meters) often develop as well as ath-

DOI: 10.4324/9781003238201-2

letes who run faster in high school, then maybe Mike wants to award one full scholarship and four half scholarships to five athletes rather than award three full scholarships to three athletes. This is a very realistic scenario and one that collegiate coaches face regularly. Hence, the context for this problem is looking at performance data for past athletes in an attempt to create a mathematical model for future athletes.

Subject Focus of the Chapter

This chapter's subject focus is on trends. Trends can be found in many places. For example, business analysts seek trends in the stock market to be able to predict what will happen in similar situations in the future. Sports and military experts seek trends to see how their competitors will react and behave given certain stimuli. Meteorologists and climatologists seek trends in an attempt to be more accurate with long-range predictions and to assist in the creation of weather/mathematical models. Retail experts seek trends to see what to order and ultimately place in stores in an attempt to have the most recent or hottest product line. It is thus not surprising that the subject of trends was selected by experts in statistics as one of the most important topics, and it is therefore the focus of the first chapter.

Links to NCTM Content Standards

This problem has many links to NCTM content standards. As a quick review, there are five content standards (NCTM, 2000). These five content areas are: algebra, data analysis and probability, geometry, measurement, and number sense and operations. It is realistic to expect that these activities will link with content standards in data analysis and probability, as per the emphasis of this book. Interestingly enough, given the open-ended nature of MEAs, many other content standards are often met, but they may not be met by all students, depending on the type of solution path selected by the group. It would be safe to assume, however, that nearly all students would meet the following NCTM content standards when completing The 10,000 Meters Problem:

- Select, create, and use appropriate graphical representations of data including histograms, box plots, and scatterplots (grade band 6–8).
- Make conjectures about possible relationships between two characteristics of a sample on the basis of scatterplots of the data and approximate lines of best fit (grade band 6–8).

- Identify trends in bivariate data and find functions that model the data or transform the data so that they can be modeled (grade band 9–12).
- Understand how sample statistics reflect the values of population parameters and use sampling distributions as the basis for informal inference (grade band 9–12).
- Understand how basic statistical techniques are used to monitor process characteristics in the workplace (grade band 9–12).

In addition, for all MEAs in this book, the algebra standard "Model and solve contextualized problems using various representations, such as graphs, tables, and equations" is met.

Questions to Pose to Students

It is important to pose questions pertinent to the implementation of the MEA to students throughout the process. For example, it is incumbent upon the instructor to ensure that students understand what is being asked in the problem statement. The most expeditious and forthright manner in which to investigate comprehension of the problem statement is to ask groups if they understand what is being asked. However, the focus of this section is not on closed-ended questions. Instead, the focus is on questions that instructors may use to serve in the role as metacognitive coach (Papinczak, 2010). It is important that instructors do not answer any questions about solving the problem. Questions about clarifying the problem can be answered, but responses to questions that *give away* part or all of the answer should be avoided at all times. In this respect, instructors are serving as metacognitive coaches by using questions to guide students' thinking (Stepien, Gallagher, & Workman, 1993). Several potential questions may arise from students. These may be referred to as "sticking points" or points in the problem when groups of students appear to reach an impasse. After repeated implementations of multiple MEAs, students rarely ask leading questions designed to retrieve a solution from an instructor because they come to the realization that instructors will not reveal answers.

Instructors will find that some general questions may be used from activity to activity, such as:
- How does that computation help you develop a mathematical model that explains the situation?
- Can you be clearer regarding the process that you used to create the model?
- How would the model change if you eliminated this procedure?

There are also questions that instructors will develop in using The 10,000 Meters Problem that are specific to this MEA. As an example, instructors may find themselves asking some of the following questions:

- Do any of the (first two) columns have anything to do with any of the other columns of data?
- Do you see any patterns in the data?
- Do any examples (i.e., individual data points, athletes) exist that might help you develop an idea about the data?
- How will your explanation help Coach Hall give out scholarships to high school athletes?
- Did you go back to read the statement to see that your final solution meets the expectations of the client (Coach Hall)?

Undoubtedly, additional questions will surface. Some may prove common to the problem, but will not appear so until the problem is implemented repeatedly.

Potential Student Responses

Given the fact that students in grades 4–6 may not completely understand how scholarships work—though some may be familiar with the process—instructors will need to check on students' final responses to see that they have grasped the concept. It is also important to note that scholarships need not be awarded in increments of 25%. A coach reserves the right to award any percent scholarship that he or she deems necessary. For instance, a coach can split a scholarship two, three, or more ways, but when the offer becomes too minimal, athletes will start to compare the offer with offers from other academic institutions.

The focus of this problem is to look at data to identify potential trends. The value in identifying trends in this instance is to be able to make more calculated, systematic, and informed decisions for the recruitment of future athletes. In creating a mathematical model to explain the data, Coach Hall will be able to use data to draw inferences (Standard 4, Links to NCTM Content Standards) to make informed decisions. From an instructor's perspective, the question remains: "What sort of potential responses may be created by students?" First, it is imperative to note that, whenever one is administering a MEA, the person administering the MEA should complete it, ideally with a peer, prior to administering it. This is highly advised because the individual administering the MEA will then have insight regarding potential problems and barriers en route to completing the problem. With a strong group of students, many responses will be created. Incumbent upon the instructor administering the MEA is the responsibility of seeking rationales for the models and identifying which ones are most mathematically efficient and sophisticated.

Potential responses to The 10,000 Meters Problem are varied and this list does not represent all potential responses; it simply presents common responses. Instructors should also seek potentially creative (i.e., novel) responses.

Solution 1

A common response to this MEA is to simply look at the final times and to select the athletes who ran the fastest times. This is not a particularly insightful answer, nor is it complete, because the old adage "hindsight is 20/20" is apropos. Ideally, the instructor would head off such a response prior to students sharing it with the larger group by asking for more specificity in the response. Telling the coach that the fastest athletes are the ones to select does not do the coach any good, nor does it meet the demands of the task, because a mathematical model that gives the coach insight regarding future athletes to recruit is not provided. In its basic element, students should look at past data and trends in an attempt to enable the coach the opportunity to identify current high school athletes to bring on to the team with scholarship offers. Hence, students must be able to identify a system that can be offered to the coach.

Solution 2

A better response than the initial one provided may occur when a group looks at the percentage change from the high school (HS) 10,000-meter time to the college 10,000-meter time. Data have deliberately been scattered so that the two relationships are not perfectly consistent with one another. This is typical of what might happen in a real-life setting. Groups must be reminded that relationships are good to seek when analyzing data for potential trends, but the ultimate goal is to provide a mathematical model for the coach so that he can identify the athletes with the most potential to run fast times throughout their college careers.

Alternatively, or in addition, a group can look at the difference between the HS 5,000-meter time and the college 10,000-meter time by using the formula *2 x HS 5000-meter time + 1 minute*. This is a formula that has been used internationally to see how fast one should be able to run if the athlete has only run the 5,000 meters and not the 10,000 meters. Instructors may choose to introduce this formula prior to the MEA or in the debriefing stage, upon conclusion. (Note, however, that a major disadvantage to introducing it prior to the MEA is that problem solvers may feel compelled to use it in their mathematical models, thus diminishing the creativity of their responses.) Although 10,000-meter times have been provided here, most high school athletes (at least in the

United States) run the 5,000 and not the 10,000 on a regular basis. This is one reason that the HS 5,000-meter times have been provided and deserve serious consideration.

For the record, if students attempt to look at the correlation between the HS 10,000-meter personal record (PR) and the college 10,000-meter PR, they will find a coefficient of .8977, which is stronger than the coefficient between the high school 5,000-meter PR and the college 10,000-meter PR (which is .8287). This is not surprising because some individuals who run fast 5,000-meter times are mile runners and not 10,000-meter runners. As such, the HS 10,000-meter time is a slightly better indicator of college 10,000-meter success than the high school 5,000-meter time is, but both are strong predictors. In either case, instructors should remember that a formal correlation is not what is sought with respect to a mathematical model in this situation.

Solution 3

Another response, not necessarily better or worse than Solution 2, is to rank order the 10,000-meter high school performances and to see how they compare to the respective 10,000-meter college performances. Similarly, this approach can be used with the HS 5,000-meter PRs and the college 10,000-meter PRs. Ranking performances is a powerful approach in statistics, but it does have some limitations. This is because it is an unsafe assumption to think that the intervals between all ranks are equal. As an example, when looking at high school PRs for 10,000 meters relative to college PRs for 10,000 meters, there is a 37-second difference between the fifth and sixth best high school PR and a 5-second difference between the fifth and sixth best college PR. Hence, the *rank-order model*, as some call it, may have some flaws and this needs to be carefully explicated as a potential shortcoming in the final explanation of the model.

For a fully detailed example of this solution, including data tables and a sample student letter to the client, see Appendix B.

Solution 4

Another approach is to analyze consistency of athletes throughout the 4-year period of college. This approach is one in which problem solvers analyze the productivity of athletes over a long period of time. The big difference between this and other responses is that this approach assumes that Coach Hall would like to have consistency over a 4-year period, which is not uncommon for most coaches. Hence, looking for consistency and relating it to performances in high school is a logical approach. However, if Mike is only concerned with the single fastest time that an athlete could run in a 4-year period, then analyzing consistency may not be particularly helpful. This consideration is a good one to bring up in post-activity discussion.

Solution 5

A stronger solution can be found by combining two or more of the previous solutions. This is how an actual statistician might solve the problem; rarely is one statistical procedure employed and found satisfactory. Often statisticians implement a statistical procedure and the results promote a question in another area. As such, one statistical procedure may well beget another procedure altogether. This may have been the case with the aforementioned solutions. It could be the case that percentage change solution precipitated thought regarding the rank-order procedure. Hence, it is possible to look at results and mathematical models from one solution and consider them in relation to another mathematical solution.

Merging solutions may also illustrate flexibility in thinking (Krutetski, 1976). Krutetski (1976) referred to the ability to look at a mathematical problem in more than one way as *flexibility*. He identified this as one of his nine ways of advanced thinking that indicate giftedness in mathematics.

Additional Responses

Naturally, additional responses exist. However, the focus of this section is on identifying common responses that may be created by students in grades 4–6. As such, the use of more sophisticated procedures that involve looking at the appearance of the data (e.g., kurtosis or skewness of a graph) as tools of analysis are not likely with students at this age. Some students may find a scatterplot to be helpful, and it is a worthwhile tool in ultimately creating a mathematical model. As with all mathematical and statistical approaches, sophisticated procedures that do not provide insight to the ultimate solution should not be used simply for the sake of using sophisticated procedures.

Notes on Implementation

Some implementation tactics are common from MEA to MEA. As with most MEAs, The 10,000 Meters Problem should require approximately 45–60 minutes to solve and students should be provided with sufficient time to document their solution process (including incorrect paths pursued). Further, ample time should be provided for student presentations. If only one group (e.g., 3–4 students) is doing the problem, presentations may not need to be formal or may not be done at all. Regarding materials, a very basic calculator will suffice for any and all computations. It is not recommended that sophisticated software be an option for groups as they may find themselves selecting features that they do not understand. Moreover, the use of a statistical procedure may solve the problem, but it does little for demanding that students create a mathematical model as a solution. Graph paper may be of use to students and instructors may find additional materials helpful. However, it is a good idea to mention what materials exist without demanding that groups use any or all of the materials. Students should not be deprived of desired materials so long as the materials help them develop a strong mathematical model. Historically, some very creative models (solutions) have been created with scant materials.

The 10,000 Meters Problem

Mike Hall is a college distance coach in track and field. In his job, he has to do several things. For example, he has to select meets for his athletes to run, arrange travel for trips, help athletes with their diets, make sure they are doing well in college classes, decide how athletes will train, and recruit athletes that he can develop into the best athletes in the United States. Unlike high school, where coaches simply work with athletes who try out for the team, college coaches can find high school athletes and encourage them to come to their college. This process is called recruiting athletes. Recruiting is a very important and difficult part of Coach Hall's job. When he gives an athlete a scholarship (i.e., money to come to his school), he will work with the athlete for the next 4–5 years, so he needs to be quite careful that he makes good decisions when giving scholarships.

Coach Hall's main responsibility is to prepare athletes to run the 10,000-meter race (approximately 6.2 miles), so he has focused his recruiting efforts in looking at athletes' 10,000-meter times. Until recently, Coach Hall had simply looked at the athlete's form and run times and made offers from these data. He had not done anything formally with the data that he found. However, recently Coach Hall has realized that there must be a more systematic way to investigate how fast athletes might be able to run by examining their high school times.

Readiness Questions

1. What is Mike Hall's job?

2. What event does Mike coach at his college?

3. About how far is 10,000 meters?

4. What does "recruiting" mean in college athletics?

5. For how many years will Mike work with an athlete that he recruits?

Data Table: Run Times

Athlete	High School 5,000-Meter PR	High School 10,000-Meter PR	College Freshman PR	College Sophomore PR	College Junior PR	College Senior PR	All-Time PR
Assefe Bekele	14:47	30:08	29:31	29:38	29:12	28:58	28:58
Mark Berkshire	16:17	DNR	32:28	32:17	32:23	31:38	31:38
Eddie Billings	16:14	33:15	32:43	32:21	31:59	31:30	31:30
Tom Brinkston	15:37	32:29	31:12	DNR	31:20	DNR	31:12
Mekonnen Demissie	14:32	30:04	29:36	29:03	28:51	28:58	28:51
Brent Doerhoffer	16:21	33:15	33:08	31:42	31:42	31:17	31:17
Moses Kigen	14:58	30:45	30:30	30:27	29:57	29:32	29:32
Michael Kipkosgei	14:18	29:45	30:03	29:58	29:03	29:12	29:03
William Kiprono	14:32	30:06	30:38	29:27	29:36	30:14	29:27
Frank Lemit	15:40	32:10	32:28	31:55	31:17	31:23	31:17
Sean McLaughlin	15:15	31:53	30:42	29:38	30:07	29:40	29:38
Robert Ngugi	15:03	32:00	31:37	31:23	DNR	30:10	30:10
Keegan O'Malley	14:54	30:03	30:00	29:43	29:12	DNR	29:12
Mel Stein	15:28	31:58	31:47	31:53	31:22	30:36	30:36
Martin Stoughlin	16:02	32:12	31:47	31:53	31:17	30:12	30:12
Dereje Tesfaye	15:21	31:54	31:54	31:37	31:43	31:10	31:10
Tim Williams	15:08	31:55	32:10	31:08	31:11	31:09	31:08

The acronym PR stands for *personal record* and it represents the fastest time that the athlete ran in that event. The acronym DNR represents the term *did not run* (typically due to injury). All college times are for 10,000 meters, and all times are in minutes and seconds.

Problem Statement

Using the data on Coach Hall's athletes provided, create a method for awarding scholarships to future athletes interested in joining the team. It is reasonable to give out two or three full scholarships per year and it is possible to give less than a full scholarship. Remember, if you give too small of a scholarship you may lose the athlete to another team, so you may want to have several levels of scholarships (e.g., 100%, 75%, 50%, 25%). Your task is to provide a rationale for awarding the scholarships. Write a detailed letter to Coach Hall showing how you decided on your rationale.

Chapter 2

Spread of Data

The Salesperson Problem

The world of business offers many opportunities for statistical applications and procedures given rather voluminous sets of data. Businesspeople base many of their decisions on summary statistics provided by statisticians. Seemingly endless scenarios exist in which businesspeople can utilize the skills of and data provided by qualified statisticians. For instance, market research (data) can have rather immediate implications for sales. Asking students to investigate statistical applications to business would be a worthy topic for students in an attempt to engage them in a discussion about business and its relationship to statistics.

A typical use of statistical procedures is to analyze quarterly sales data. The results from these analyses can be used to make decisions in several areas. For example, businesspeople may decide to target a new geographic area for product distribution and sales if data look promising. Another use of data is to investigate the performance (i.e., sales volume) of salespeople in an attempt to create mathematical models for pay structures. Still another use is to analyze data from sales to see which salespeople should be retained and which salespeople should be eliminated. This last example is the focus of the MEA for this chapter. In The Salesperson Problem, students are asked to identify a means by which to analyze data with an emphasis on consistency in sales. As a quick example, a salesperson with the highest sales ever recorded in a quarter, but with a very large range of sales data, might not be as desirable as a salesperson with a high degree of consistency in sales data (assuming that data is sufficiently high). This problem has a focus on more than just looking at ranges of performance in sales (data), however. Looking merely at the range of data in

DOI: 10.4324/9781003238201-3

sales is a very entry-level approach and students advanced in mathematics in grades 4–6 are highly capable of developing more sophisticated mathematical models.

In this activity, students are presented with the sales data of 20 individuals for 8 quarters (or 2 full years). These individuals sell T-shirts, which is of interest to Belle Dunkirk, the client for The Salesperson Problem. Belle, a junior high student, is interested in starting her own T-shirt company. She has had success in the past selling T-shirts to peers at school and she thinks that if she could formalize the company, it could be a success. However, her uncle has encouraged her to look at some data from a much larger T-shirt company in an attempt to see if she can handle the rigors of the business world (e.g., hiring and firing employees based on performance).

Subject Focus of the Chapter

The answer to many statistical problems is based on a surprisingly elementary yet highly powerful concept called *spread of data*. At its heart, spread of data is related to the concept of range. Range speaks of the difference in the lowest number in the data set to the largest number in the data set plus one. However, range and spread are not perfectly synonymous terms. Range is but one component of spread. More specifically, the spread of data is the *complexion* (i.e., appearance) of the data. Statisticians are known to pose questions such as, "What is the appearance of the data?" or "What does the data look like?" To a novice, these questions may seem silly. Data do not have appearances, but when graphed, they do hold some form. For instance, data may be largely flat (i.e., no major bumps in the data), it may have more than one mode (i.e., the most frequently occurring piece of data), it may be skewed one way or another (i.e., positively or negatively), and it may have several other characteristics. As with trends, conceptually understanding spread of data is instrumental to understanding increasingly complex statistical concepts.

Links to NCTM Content Standards

Like The 10,000 Meters Problem, this activity has several links to NCTM standards. To reiterate a point made in Chapter 1, it is difficult to guarantee that all of these standards will be met by all pupils given the open-ended nature of MEAs. Given the fact that not every group will solve each MEA in precisely the same manner, it is difficult to ascertain precisely which NCTM standards will be met. In fact, if all groups solve an MEA with precisely the same mathematical model, it is typically the case that the instructor provided too much information prior to the activity. In these instances, instructors need to realize that a good deal of the learning occurs when students actually create their own mathematical models as opposed to simply implementing an established algorithm. The NCTM standards that link most closely to commonly provided models for the problem are listed below.

For The Salesperson Problem, nearly all students will meet the following NCTM content standards:

- Select, create, and use appropriate graphical representations of data including histograms, box plots, and scatterplots (grade band 6–8).
- Discuss and understand the correspondence between data sets and their graphical representations, especially histograms, stem-and-leaf plots, box plots, and scatterplots (grade band 6–8).
- Compute basic statistics and understand the distinction between a statistic and a parameter (grade band 9–12).
- Understand histograms, parallel box plots, and scatterplots and use them to display data (grade band 9–12).
- Understand how basic statistical techniques are used to monitor process characteristics in the workplace (grade band 9–12).

In addition, for all MEAs in this book, the algebra standard "Model and solve contextualized problems using various representations, such as graphs, tables, and equations" is met.

Questions to Pose to Students

To reiterate several points from Chapter 1, it is crucial that, while using questions to help students think about and understand the problem, teachers nevertheless do everything possible to not give away answers. The use of questions during the implementation of MEAs can be an indicator as to the success of the problem. Moreover, it has been speculated that the better the questions that are posed, the better the models groups will develop. Consequently, designing questions in anticipation of specific cognitive barriers may be one of the most important duties for instructors implementing any MEA.

Questions germane to The Salesperson Problem include the following:

- What does the problem statement prompt you to do?
- Are you considering both the consistency and the performance of salespeople? (A follow-up question to the first one)
- How does the process that you just completed inform you about the performance or consistency of the salespeople?

- Are the money differences the same between intervals? If not, how does that impact the model that you are creating?
- What will your model ultimately explain?
- Have you thought about the relationship between the performance and the consistency of the salespeople?
- Are there any other ways to analyze performance of salespeople?
- Are there any other ways to analyze consistency of salespeople?
- Do any faults exist in rank ordering salespeople?
- Is this the most comprehensive model that you can create?

Potential Student Responses

This problem should capture students' attention because it pertains to generating income, which is a topic that kids, even at this age, typically find interesting. Although students in grades 4–6 probably will not have had previous business experience, they are often interested in how money can be made because by this point they realize that having access to money enables the opportunity to buy and acquire goods and services.

In this situation the client, Belle Dunkirk, is interested in opening a T-shirt business. However, Belle does not have access to previous data of salespeople so she needs to rely on data provided by her uncle. Her uncle has provided data from a real T-shirt company so that she might begin to understand some of the complexity in the mathematics involved in running a business. In addition, he has encouraged her to investigate a process for keeping or eliminating future salespeople. Thus, a mathematical model needs formulating.

Naturally, anyone implementing any MEA should solve it prior to administering it. Instructors should heed one admonition when looking at students' responses. Simply identifying ranges of sales performance is an incomplete response for several reasons. Perhaps the most significant reason that a group cannot simply identify ranges and then rank order them is because all ranges are not equivalent. As an example, a range of $100 for a salesperson with a maximum number of sales of $400 differs from someone who has a range of $100 with maximum sales of $2,100: The percentage of sales relative to the overall, or composite, sales is a much smaller percentage in the second scenario. It is therefore easy to suggest that a range be used to analyze the data and create a model, but specificity must be provided with respect to the ranges of the salespeople in the mathematical model. The variety of the data is what makes the use of ranges somewhat problematic in this instance, though the use of range is a powerful statistical tool.

For this activity, six responses are provided. The first three are fairly common responses, but the instructor should think about what questions can be posed to help the students refine their answers. This is because the first three responses are not particularly comprehensive responses. The next two solutions are decent, though not terribly creative. The final response is very strong, as it provides a rationale that is fairly sophisticated in statistics.

Solution 1

The first solution that is somewhat typical is for a group or groups of students to simply look at the range and then rank order the salespeople. Alternatively, some students will simply look at the overall (i.e., composite) sales and rank order them. Composite sales can be formulated by adding the total sales for the eight quarters for each individual. Once the composites have been computed, students can rank order the salespeople based on the composite sales of each employee.

The reason that rank ordering the ranges or the overall sales is an entry-level solution is because the problem statement asks groups to look at the data with two measures of evaluation in mind. Solvers are asked to consider the performance of the salespeople (typically measured by how well or poorly they have done in overall sales) while also looking at the consistency of their sales. Hence, analyzing either one exclusively is not a comprehensive solution.

On a side note, it is important to point out that computing an arithmetic mean, while not an incorrect approach to this solution, is not necessary, as all of the participants had data for each quarter. In computing an arithmetic mean, groups will be adding an unnecessary step to the solution process. This is because when one divides all of the composites by 8 (the number of quarters), all of the data will stay in the same order as the summation of data, as they are all being divided by a constant.

Solution 2

Another solution that is not particularly comprehensive is to simply look at other measures of central tendency (e.g., median or mode) and render a decision. The reason that this solution is not comprehensive is because the problem asks solvers to consider consistency, which these measures, used alone, are not helpful for analyzing. Solvers should have a rationale for using measures of central tendency. These measures will be the focus of the next chapter.

Solution 3

Some groups may use the standard deviation (SD) formula as their mathematical model. This is not inappropriate, but using the SD alone will precipitate the same problem that Solutions 1 and 2 created: That is to say, the SD does not enable the group to look at how consistently the salespeople have performed in overall sales. It is a strong indicator of range, and perhaps best suited to explicate range, but it does not detail the overall sales of respective salespeople. (Teachers unfamiliar with the SD procedure may want to take this time to look at the glossary, or ahead to Chapter 3, where the SD is explained in greater detail.)

Furthermore, if a group at this age range uses standard deviation, we must ask the question: *Do they conceptually understand what a standard deviation is?* Students may find it intriguing to use a sophisticated procedure, but they may not understand if the procedure is appropriate or the most informative. In essence, they may just be using the procedure to use the procedure and to impress peers. However, sophisticated procedures are not helpful if they provide inaccurate, inadequate, or incomplete information. Hence, instructors should feel compelled, as with all MEAs, to ask probing questions regarding *why* groups selected specific procedures. Another manner in which to think about this issue is to demand that groups provide rationales for their mathematical decisions.

Solution 4

A more comprehensive solution than the previous three would be to first look at and rank order the composite sales. Then, the group can look at the range for each salesperson in relation to the overall sales. The group can then look at the range (numerator) relative to the composite sales (denominator) to attain a fraction that can be expressed as a percentage. From these two pieces of data (i.e., the rank order of the composite sales and the rank order of the percentage of range relative to composite sales), the group can then formulate a decision with a strong mathematical model.

For example, Ellen's composite sales total is $12,578.38, and she displays a range of $2,78.67. Dividing the range into the composite total produces a value of 0.02215, or about 2.22%. Charles, on the other hand, had $11,484.91 in composite sales, with a range of $445.89. His percentage, therefore, is 3.88%. Ellen's lower percentage value indicates that she is the more consistent salesperson of the two. This process, when applied to the entire data set, would make for a powerful, complete mathematical model.

Solution 5

The fifth solution is very similar to Solution 4; however, in this instance the standard deviation process (see Solution 3) is used in lieu of the range relative to composite sales. The rank order changes somewhat when using the SD. Groups may use these two pieces of data to formulate a decision. It is important that at least two pieces of data be used to formulate a decision because the final question asks solvers to look at both the salespeople's overall performance and their consistency.

Solution 6

Solution 6 is a combination of the previous two responses and is consequently the most comprehensive of all of the given solutions. Here, students would first compute the overall sales and rank order the salespeople. Next, students would look at the range relative to the composite sales and create a percentage. This can then be used to rank order the salespeople. Third, students would compute the standard deviation and rank order the salespeople once more. The caveat with using these three pieces of data is that two of the pieces of data have an emphasis on consistency (measured by range) and the other component (overall sales) is only considered in one situation. It can be argued that consistency is considered twice because the second piece of data is a percentage of the range relative to the overall sales.

An important point to remember when dealing with any solution that includes rank ordering is that some issues may arise regarding the equivalency of ranks. For example, if the following ranks are attained, then all intervals are not considered equally:

Overall sales
4. Kristi: $13,939.99
5. Abioye: $13,929.22
6. Cody: $13,143.31

Kristi and Abioye are only $10.77 apart in sales (one ranking) and Abioye and Cody are $785.91 apart in sales (one ranking). Hence, all intervals are not the same, even though a ranking might imply that they are.

Notes on Implementation

Some background knowledge of the business world will likely need to be reviewed or introduced prior to The Salesperson Problem. This information need not be in great detail as the context of the problem should not be particularly foreign to students in grades 4–6. Though it is unlikely any of the students have ever operated a business, the basic tenets of The Salesperson Problem are not complex. Essentially, all students need to realize what a sales quarter is (i.e., a 3-month period, or one fourth of a year). They should also realize that there are situations in which some employees may need to be let go and therefore having a mathematical model to identify the top salespeople is critical to the success of a business. Finally, it should be explained that individuals with high sales one quarter and poor sales the next might not be as valuable as more consistent salespeople with lesser peak sales quarters.

It is necessary for this and for all MEAs that students have two types of knowledge. First, it is integral that students have ample mathematical knowledge, conceptually and procedurally, to solve each problem. Asking students to solve a task that is years in excess of their knowledge is not a desirable situation from a developmental or affective position. The second type of knowledge that is necessary for success is a strong understanding of the context. With The Salesperson Problem, students may require a small amount of review or introduction of business conventions to be able to solve the problem, though this knowledge is not excessive. If an instructor finds him- or herself stopping repeatedly to review contextual information, then the setup of the MEA was insufficient.

If either knowledge base is lacking, success will be compromised because the teacher will not have placed the students in a position to create a mathematical model.

The Salesperson Problem

Belle Dunkirk is thinking about starting a small company to sell T-shirts. Her uncle owns a rotary garment screen-printing machine that she can use to print designs. He's offered to print as many shirts for her as she'd like, and he can print them very quickly. He's even managed to help Belle get a discount on the T-shirts she buys, so she won't have to sell very many to make a profit. Her plan is to print new T-shirts and wear them to school, to see if her classmates like them. When she gets enough interest in a certain design, she will print some T-shirts up and sell them.

She has several friends in her junior high school who want to help her with the business. She'll need someone in charge of marketing and advertising, so that people know about her products. She'll also need someone to deliver T-shirts ordered from her website, someone to keep track of the money she makes, and a few people to actually help her sell the shirts.

Belle is concerned with finding qualified salespeople. Specifically, she is concerned with what qualities she should seek when hiring salespeople. Successful salespeople may be the most important part of her business, and she wants salespeople who are self-sufficient and do not need help from her. Two things that she keeps considering are (a) what makes a salesperson successful and (b) how important consistency in sales is to her business.

After talking to a few friends and relatives, she has found that some salespeople show more fluctuations in sales than others. Some people do much better at different times of the year, whereas others show very little change from month to month or quarter to quarter. (Note: A quarter is one fourth of the year, or 3 months. Not all companies start and finish quarters at the same time.)

Readiness Questions

1. What are three responsibilities that Belle will have in her company?

2. What does Belle want to use the rotary garment screen-printing machine for?

3. What is one characteristic that Belle is seeking in a salesperson?

4. How long is a quarter, in the sales world?

5. How will Belle decide whether or not to print up a T-shirt design?

Data Table: T-Shirt Sales

Salesperson	Q1	Q2	Q3	Q4	Q5	Q6	Q7	Q8
Ellen	1438.27	1514.78	1658.23	1543.22	1499.34	1716.94	1515.32	1692.28
Charles	1328.66	1329.45	1412.58	1587.73	1268.44	1319.91	1714.33	1523.81
Marcus	1562.34	1672.81	958.21	1784.29	1633.72	1684.56	1012.89	1227.73
Jeff	857.45	912.55	1145.71	1342.88	1400.19	1474.86	1508.23	1555.82
Ruth	1574.33	1523.47	1601.45	1538.29	1454.79	1488.61	1567.11	1478.64
LeShawn	1268.47	1792.45	1654.73	849.52	900.12	1456.32	1678.24	1158.37
Abioye	1878.65	1674.39	1948.38	1649.00	1756.10	1508.32	1629.71	1884.61
Vladimir	1908.76	1875.24	1655.32	1840.92	1950.43	1712.93	1681.93	1858.19
Michael	1733.24	1786.57	1534.43	1650.19	1492.57	1398.85	1312.45	1567.31
Kristi	1987.45	1945.32	1898.57	1950.19	1617.83	1451.89	1564.84	1523.90
Julie	1378.61	1488.11	1674.04	1324.81	987.65	1145.31	891.35	1567.21
Pete	912.56	1014.77	984.56	1267.51	1489.31	874.15	1385.14	1464.22
Harold	1546.32	1678.22	1319.41	312.71	618.97	1498.01	1134.67	1876.51
Milhouse	1546.32	1498.63	1523.77	456.78	1587.02	1467.11	1459.03	512.74
Dana	1254.38	1319.00	1167.89	1201.45	1354.77	1468.23	1350.19	1500.92
Cody	1609.34	1863.26	1783.45	1492.58	1600.01	1557.83	1756.18	1480.66
Xavier	1876.54	2109.47	1934.10	1839.88	1764.82	1984.35	1872.01	1778.11
Katie	965.78	1012.82	1066.45	1190.16	1050.67	1236.90	1312.74	1456.17
Trigger	1789.53	1623.71	2012.88	1319.03	1985.28	1902.58	1649.51	1712.60
Ed	1327.88	1598.64	1438.73	1253.79	1451.02	1667.33	1728.34	1434.77

Q = Quarter (i.e., 3 months, or one fourth of the calendar year). All numbers are in U.S. dollars: For example, the number 1438.27 represents $1,438.27. This number means that in the first 3 months of the calendar year, Ellen sold $1,438.27 worth of T-shirts for her company.

Problem Statement

Belle is starting a company to print, sell, and distribute T-shirts. She wants her company to be successful. Therefore, she needs sales to be consistent. This is because she needs to have a dependable amount of money each month so that she can make plans for the amount of money she can spend the next month.

Belle's uncle has provided her with some sales data from a major national T-shirt company. He hopes that it might help her determine how to select salespeople for her company. She is having a hard time, however, making sense of the data. Using the table provided, write a letter to Belle Dunkirk explaining how you would select the best and most consistent salespeople for her T-shirt company. Invest specific attention in seeing how consistent salespeople are from quarter to quarter and also pay attention to the dollar amount of sales. In other words, if one salesperson has consistent sales at a certain amount (e.g., $1,350) and another salesperson has inconsistent sales at the same amount ($1,350), you should retain the person with the more consistent record of sales. In your letter, make a recommendation regarding the top 10 salespeople you would keep, explain your process to Belle, and provide your reasons for keeping them.

Chapter **3**

Measures of Central Tendency

The Taxicab Problem

In very large cities, many people do not own cars due to excessive costs. Paying for fuel on a weekly basis, car maintenance at regular intervals, and parking every evening, week, month, or year can become rather cost prohibitive, so many people forego ownership of a vehicle. Individuals without a car can therefore be quite reliant on taxis or other types of public transportation.

Taking a taxi is a fairly efficient, albeit sometimes expensive, mode of transportation. Despite the costs, taxis provide advantages over driving on one's own or taking the city bus or train. One advantage is that a map or GPS is not needed to decide how to get from destination to destination. The taxi driver is responsible for the safe delivery of the passenger. Taxi drivers are also intimately acquainted with the city, and can provide helpful information. If a passenger is interested in the best pizza restaurant in town, the taxi driver may have such information. And one need not be concerned with finding a parking place because no car is parked at the destination. In short, taking a taxi may not be as costly as some think!

Typically, getting picked up on time is not a concern, either, but it can be in certain situations. This problem's main consideration is whether taxi companies have varied reliability, or if all taxi companies are consistently on time. Several factors may impact promptness. In some instances, taxis and their drivers are simply waiting for customers (e.g., the taxis at many major airports). In other instances, a taxi may need to be called to a destination in order to pick up a passenger. Taking both situations into account, students will be asked to set up a mathematical model that compares the promptness of different taxicab companies, in an effort to determine which is the most reliable.

DOI: 10.4324/9781003238201-4

Subject Focus of the Chapter

The central focus of this problem is getting students to consider measures of central tendency and learning which one to use in which situations. (To some, this is called becoming a *consumer* of measures of central tendency.) Problem solvers can consider the different measures of central tendency, as well as measures of spread (as examined in the previous chapter). They should also consider using more than one measure of central tendency simultaneously to create a mathematical model as an appropriate means of completing this activity.

It could be argued that measures of central tendency is the most overused and poorest understood topic in statistics. A casual perusal of grade 3–8 textbooks would substantiate the claim that it is *covered* in every grade. Despite repeated exposure to the concept of measures of central tendency, students may exhibit very little understanding of the topic and would therefore be poor consumers of information. As proof, one could ask students which measure—median, mean, or mode—should be used to summarize data. Students are often capable of regurgitating textbook and classroom definitions of such measures, but they may not always possess intimate knowledge of what each represents. Instructors should pay close attention to what measures the students are employing, and use the debriefing discussion following completion of the activity as a time to get students to justify why they employed their chosen techniques, and what information each actually provides in context of the problem.

Closely tied to measures of central tendency is the concept of standard deviation (SD). Students at this age should not be expected to know what a SD is, but because SD is an appropriate means of formulating a solution to this problem, the instructor may want to consider using the postactivity debriefing period as a time to introduce students to the SD process.

If students are familiar with it and would like to use it with this problem, the instructor should make sure that they understand what it actually represents, and not just simply compute it (such is the case whenever students opt to use the SD or any other statistical procedure).

Links to NCTM Content Standards

An inherent quality of all MEAs is that they contain more than one solution. In that respect, The Taxicab Problem is consistent with all MEAs. Many authentic mathematical problems (Chamberlin, 2011) have more than one solution (process), but not more than one product (final response). An interesting aspect of this problem is that there is clearly more than one solution and prospectively more than one product. For this reason, it is difficult to guarantee that all standards will be met by all students. The standards listed are those that will likely be accomplished by the vast majority of students. Ascertaining standards is typically problematic for all students when highly open-ended problems are implemented in mathematics. To reiterate a statement proposed in Chapter 2, if all groups solve an MEA with precisely the same mathematical model, it is likely the case that the instructor provided too much information prior to the activity or that the MEA was poorly constructed.

For The Taxicab Problem, nearly all students will meet the following NCTM content standards:

- Find, use, and interpret measures of center and spread, including mean and interquartile range (grade band 6–8).
- Discuss and understand the correspondence between data sets and their graphical representations, especially histograms, stem-and-leaf plots, box plots, and scatterplots (grade band 6–8).
- Use observations about differences between two or more samples to make conjectures about the populations from which the samples were taken (grade band 6–8).
- Compute basic statistics and understand the distinction between a statistic and a parameter (grade band 9–12).
- Identify trends in bivariate data and find functions that model the data or transform the data so that they can be modeled (grade band 9–12).
- Understand how sample statistics reflect the values of population parameters and use sampling distributions as the basis for informal inference (grade band 9–12).

In addition, for all MEAs in this book, the algebra standard "Model and solve contextualized problems using various representations, such as graphs, tables, and equations" is met.

Questions to Pose to Students

As with all MEAs, there are questions with universal applicability that are appropriate to use here, and there are questions that are germane to this activity that are not relevant to other MEAs. It is significant to reiterate that a requisite component to facilitate success in all MEAs, however, is the successful use of teacher questions during implementation. Teachers should serve as metacognitive coaches in that they should pose questions to help students clarify their thinking and their mathematical models, but they must not overtly convey answers or mathematical models. The term *elicit* is crucial when making mathematical models and students need to create mathematical models rather than regurgitate models that a teacher tells them. Simply recording mathematical models presented by teachers does not precipitate cognition and it thwarts creativity.

Questions pertinent to The Taxicab Problem include the following:

- Why are you using the arithmetic mean (or median, or mode) instead of a different measure of central tendency?
- What does the standard deviation actually mean in this problem?
- Have you considered using more than one measure (e.g., measure of spread or central tendency) to create your mathematical model?
- Should you simply neglect a statistic if it was not informative (e.g., the mean) or could you perhaps use it later in your model?
- In considering the several models that you've proposed, which one seems to provide the most detailed analysis of the data set?
- What does using a frequency count tell you about the companies and the data?
- Do outliers impact your mathematical model and findings at all?
- Would the creation of a table help you organize your data more efficiently than you currently have it organized?

Potential Student Responses

It may be common for students to see a long list of data and to automatically seek the arithmetic mean of the data. Not surprisingly, with this data set the arithmetic mean is modestly different for several companies, but it is insufficient to be able to select a company that has the greatest likelihood of being on time. Hence, several alternate solutions, of varying degrees of correctness, are ideal for this MEA. This MEA is one of the most interesting of all MEAs in this book due to the large number of responses that students may generate.

Solution 1

As stated in the previous paragraph, a natural inclination for mathematical problem solvers is to create an arithmetic mean from the data. Dr. Richard Lesh, professor of mathematics education at Indiana University and the man credited with creating and popularizing MEAs, was notorious for stating, "Give a set of numbers to some problem solvers and they'll find the (arithmetic) mean of them" (personal communication, February 8, 2001). He hypothesized that problem solvers would do this regardless of the problem statement. Incidentally, anecdotal data suggests that he is correct about this outcome. Computing the mean for this problem is certainly not an incorrect approach, and it is arguably the most natural starting point. However (and not incidentally, as the data were intentionally created by the author), the arithmetic means for this problem are almost identical from company to company. In fact, the arithmetic means range from 3.275 (for Punctual Taxi and Windy City Taxi Service) to 3.625 (for Fuchsia Cab). In short, the actual difference in arrival, using only the mean, is 0.35 of a minute, or 21 seconds. To the client with a stopwatch, this is a noticeable difference. However, to an average client simply waiting for a taxi, practically speaking 21 seconds is not noticeable. Therefore, although the arithmetic mean is a common solution to this problem, it is an insufficient solution. Students need to be able to use Polya's (1945) fourth step to mathematical problem solving, which necessitates that they look back to see that the response to the mathematical problem makes sense. With negligible differences in time (quite literally only a few seconds), it is unlikely that a statistically significant difference exists in the solution presented by computing the arithmetic mean. Therefore, another more complete solution is necessary.

Solution 2

Faced with feedback from the teacher that indicates that the mean is an insufficient mathematical model for this problem, students are faced with the task of creating another model. An impulse may be to identify another measure of central tendency. It is not uncommon for students to learn the measures of central tendency in the order of mean, median, and mode. Consequently, many individuals will seek the median, and it is imperative that teachers ask students why they are using the median. Suggesting that the mean was not sufficiently informative to answer the question is not an ideal response to accept. However, the medians for this problem are, respectively, 1, 0, 0.5, 1, and 3. Again, the data have been created intentionally so that looking at the median is not particularly helpful. This has been done because simply computing a measure of central tendency (e.g., mean, median, or mode) is not a strong mathematical model when used without meaning attached to the measure. Interestingly enough, the medians are very similar, but if a group starts to consider the mean in relation to the median, Punctual Taxi starts to emerge as a viable selection. This approach (i.e., using both the mean and median together) makes for a strong mathematical model. This is because Punctual Taxi had the lowest mean and it had the lowest median. Considering one measure in relation to another is a process that can be considered a mathematical model. Nevertheless, some groups will realize that no real statistical importance is attained in looking at the median because four of the companies have medians within one second given the range of 0–1.

Solution 3

It is hoped that analyzing the mean and the median might precipitate a desire to investigate the mode. Should groups be interested in the mode, they should be prompted to reiterate what the mode actually is. Some groups will regurgitate a textbook definition such as, *The mode is the most frequently occurring number in the data set*. This is a good place to start because group members will be able to identify the number of minutes late that occurs most frequently for all taxi companies. Not surprisingly, however, the modes are all the same for all of the companies in the data set. Each company has a mode of 0, which means that if a group uses the most frequently occurring number as the average, then 0 is the response for all companies. Thus, the mode as an indicator of average is not a particularly helpful statistical tool.

Solution 4

At this point, some groups will come to the realization that the data have been intentionally cooked up so that the previously discussed measures of central tendency are not particularly useful. This is not completely untrue. Groups are now faced with making a decision between two options. First, groups may opt to discard the measures of central tendency altogether. Second, they may salvage the work already done and see if the measures can be put to good use. This proves problematic for many groups because it is not atypical for students to simply have to compute the measures of central tendency and to regurgitate them on a test or on a homework assignment. Finding a successful link between using the measures or finding them unhelpful and discarding them may hinge upon the implementation of a creative response. A creative response may be to look at all of the measures simultaneously by perhaps creating a table rating all companies on all measures. An example is shown below.

	Fuchsia Cab	Punctual Taxi	Rush Street Taxi	Emergency Taxi Service	Windy City Taxi Service
Mean	5	1 (tie)	4	3	1 (tie)
Median	3 (tie)	1	2	3 (tie)	5
Mode	1 (tie)	1 (tie)	1 (tie)	1 (tie)	1 (tie)

If groups decide to compare all three measures and they create some sort of ranking such as the one shown above, they have created a mathematical model. A more sophisticated approach to this problem, however, is to consider the interval in each ranking. In other words, is the interval between the first and second rankings of any measure the same as the interval between the third and fourth rankings? This is not typically the case when data sets are assigned a ranking based on position. That said, it is fairly easy to see that Punctual Taxi does rank first in all categories and could therefore be considered a very safe selection in identifying the company most likely to be on time.

Solution 5

Another mathematical model is to consider a measure of spread. For students in grades 4–6, the range is perhaps the measure of spread that is most comfortable to use. Combining the range with one or more of the measures of central tendency has the potential to create a fairly powerful mathematical model. When discussing the range, solvers should realize that the lowest time for all companies is 0 minutes late and the greatest time for any company is a full 60 minutes late (Punctual Taxi). Hence, the range for Punctual Taxi is 0–60, or 61 total minutes.

Other measures of spread that may be used (but would require graphs or statistical computations) might be things such as kurtosis or skew. These can be informative, but they may not be the best mathematical models for this particular problem and they are seldom discussed in young grades.

Solution 6

Similar to a mode is a frequency count. A frequency count varies from a simple mode in that, instead of counting only the most commonly occurring data point, instances of occurrence are counted for all unique data points in the series. With this information, windows of data (in this case, punctuality—e.g., 0–5 minutes late, 5–10 minutes late) may be observed. A stem-and-leaf plot or some other type of graphic analysis can then be constructed with the data.

Groups may opt to operationally define "late" as something like 0–4 minutes, going on the premise that not everyone's watch is exactly the same. In effect, a client may be assuming that if a taxi is desired at 9:30 at night, then the window of 9:30 to 9:34 is acceptably on time. Thus, creating windows of "on-timeness" or punctuality is not only a practical, but also a logical, mathematical approach. The secondary window may be 5–10 minutes, the third window may be 11–20 minutes, and the fourth window might be greater than 20 minutes. As with the range, the windows of acceptance can be operationally defined from group to group. If more than one group utilizes this approach, it may be informative to compare their data to see how and why their final responses differ.

Solution 7

A final solution that would provide a strong mathematical model would be to compute the standard deviation. To compute a standard deviation, one simply needs to complete the following six steps:

1. Compute the arithmetic mean of the data set.
2. Find deviations of all data points from the mean. (For example, if the mean equals 6, a data point with a value of 3 would be -3 from the mean.)
3. Square all deviations in the data set so that they are positive.
4. Sum up all of the deviations that have been squared.
5. Divide the summed deviations by the number of data points (N) in the set or by one less data point than is in the set $(n-1)$.
6. Compute the square root of the figure from Step 5.

Concerning Step 5, debate exists among statisticians as to whether N or $(n-1)$ should be used to compute the standard deviation. Agreement has generally been reached on using N to compute the standard deviation for a population and $(n-1)$ for the sample.

It should be noted that some MEA experts question whether or not the implementation of a formula truly constitutes a successful solution for a MEA (Lesh & Caylor, 2007). To clarify, there is no doubt that a SD is a mathematical model, but some MEA developers question whether its use should be accepted as a final product when the *creation* of a mathematical model is the goal of successfully completing MEAs. The decision as to whether a SD is an acceptable solution is a local one, made by the instructors implementing the problem. The SD, however, remains a strong mathematical model, although its use should not be expected of students who have not been formally introduced to it. As this is perhaps the most appropriate problem to use the SD with, instructors should consider introducing it to the students during the debriefing period if they find that their students are not familiar with it.

Outliers

When looking at a data set such as this one, it may be informative to capitalize on the opportunity to discuss outliers. Not coincidentally, several outliers were conveniently placed in this data set to see if students would take them into account in the models that they develop. As an example, in the 13th row of afternoon data, Fuchsia Cab, Punctual Taxi, and Rush Street Taxi had outliers of 45, 60, and 35 minutes, respectively. It may be that there was excessive traffic at that time and that the other two companies already had taxicabs waiting in the areas requested. The reason for the delay is not important insomuch as the delay in arrival is worthy of note.

When faced with the concept of an outlier, students may wonder what statistically constitutes an outlier. This is a good question and it can be answered either informally or formally. At this grade range, many teachers (and, consequently, their students) will simply explain conceptually that an outlier is a piece of data that does not fit with the other data. Additional explanation is necessary because this conceptual definition is incomplete. Data sets and statistical examples can be utilized to help the teacher clearly explain the matter. Alternatively, the formal statistical procedure can be used. It is important to note that more than one agreed-upon technique exists to ascertain quantitatively whether a data point is an outlier. However, an often-used procedure is as follows:

- Line up the data from smallest to greatest.
- Find the median. With an even number of data points such as 32, one can simply divide the data set in half (i.e., 16 data points on one side and 16 on the other). The median is exactly halfway between points 16 and 17. With an odd number of data points such as 33, one simply needs to identify the data point that perfectly bisects the data (in this case, data point 17).
- Once a median has been created, create medians from the two remaining data sets. This gives the problem solver four equally distributed data sets known as interquartiles.
- To ascertain whether a data point is a statistical outlier, subtract the first interquartile from the third interquartile, to get an interquartile deviation, and see if the potential outlier is more than 1.5 interquartile deviations from the data set. If it is more than 1.5 interquartile deviations from the data set, it is considered an outlier by most definitions.

Notes on Implementation

The idea of taking a taxicab may be foreign to some students, but most if not all students have at least seen one on television, on the Internet, or in a movie. Consequently, they can understand the premise behind taking a taxi from one point to another as a means of transportation. Also, the notion of trying to identify the taxicab company that is most prompt should not be foreign to students. As stated in previous chapters, a deep familiarity with the identified MEA is necessary prior to implementation. Once the problem has been read in detail and solved as many ways as possible by the teacher, several implementation techniques may be helpful.

For instance, students must make the realization that they need to operationally define what it means to be "on time." It is not suggested that this concept be discussed overtly with the entire class. Instead, teachers can field the question as interaction unfolds. Some students will use the default (i.e., that on time is exactly 0 minutes late), and others will use more liberal measures (e.g., that on time is within 2, 3, or 4 minutes of when the taxi reported that it would arrive). It is also important to note that if groups use various operational definitions of what constitutes being on time, different models will likely come about from group to group.

Another consideration in implementing The Taxicab Problem is that often groups will conduct one computation and use it whether or not the statistic computed is actually informative. As an example, groups regularly compute the arithmetic mean for this problem and then make a selection based on the result. As a facilitator, it is imperative to help students realize the impracticality of the result when it is not a helpful stand-alone statistic. It may be helpful when used in coordination with one or more additional statistics. Further, students should realize, perhaps with help from the facilitator at the end of the problem and during the discussion, that statistical procedures are similar to a carpenter's tools. One carpenter may use one tool in one situation and another carpenter may use an altogether different tool in the same situation. Moreover, some carpenters select tools and subsequently come to the realization that the selected tool was probably not the best one to select. Hence, a carpenter who selects an unhelpful tool may go back to the toolbox to get a different tool in hopes that it will successfully help complete the job. This is an almost perfect parallel with statistical tools or procedures. It may seem obvious to use one tool (e.g., it may seem logical to use the arithmetic mean) given a data set, but when the mean is not all that informative, it may be time to identify an alternate tool that is perhaps more informative.

Finally, instructors should note that the symbol $\bar{x}$ is often used to denote arithmetic means of samples, such as are used in the MEAs in this book (μ is used to indicate means of populations, which are not tackled here). You may choose to introduce and use this symbol with your students at your discretion.

The Taxicab Problem

Brian Heder and his brother, Dave, recently moved to Chicago, IL. Brian is the manager of a famous pizza chain there, and Dave has just been hired to be a copilot for an airline at Midway International Airport. Before moving, the two debated where they should live. Brian wanted to be able to walk to work. Therefore, the two decided to live downtown, to be near Brian's workplace. The airport, however, is very far from downtown, but because Dave does not work every day of the week, and is often gone for several days at a time, he can live with the inconvenience of the commute.

Since moving, the two have decided that owning a car is not financially worth the investment and cost required to maintain, park, and operate it in the city. Chicago parking rates are notorious for being some of the most expensive in the nation. For instance, in 2012, the median daily parking rate was $35 and the monthly median rate was $289 (Colliers International, 2012). For an entire year, paying to park a car could easily run in excess of $3,500, and this is not considering any instances in which the car would need to be parked at another location such as at a restaurant or at the airport when Dave travels there to work. Coupled with very high gas prices and tolls on many roads, Chicago is an example of a city in which car ownership can get very costly in a short period of time.

For at least their first year in Chicago, Brian and Dave have decided to use public transit such as the Chicago Transit Authority bus and train system as well as the Metra and the South Shore train systems to get around the Chicago metropolitan area. In addition, they will use several taxicab companies throughout the year on an as-needed basis. They are trying to avoid using taxis excessively, due to cost, but when they use them they would like to know that the taxis are reliable. When Dave uses a taxi to go to the airport for work, it is incredibly important that the taxicab company gets him there on time. Delays of 15 to 30 minutes can be costly and make an entire jet of passengers late for takeoff. Dave copilots a Boeing 747 that seats more than 500 passengers for international flights and arriving on time is crucial to his job performance ratings. Moreover, Dave needs to be at work on time so that he can make it through security to get to his jet before scheduled departure. There are many taxicab companies in the city of Chicago and Dave has collected some data online to analyze the dependability of each company.

Readiness Questions

1. What forms of transportation are available in large cities?

2. Why are some forms of transportation used more regularly than others?

3. Why doesn't everyone in large cities own a car?

4. What type of job does Dave Heder have?

5. Why is arriving on time incredibly important to him?

Data Table: Taxicab Arrival Times

Time of Day	Fuchsia Cab	Punctual Taxi	Rush Street Taxi	Emergency Taxi Service	Windy City Taxi Service
Morning	0	4	0	10	5
	1	0	0	10	3
	0	6	4	0	1
	0	0	0	0	0
	20	0	1	3	4
	0	5	3	5	0
	12	0	2	0	7
	6	0	0	1	3
	1	0	0	1	1
	4	0	2	2	7
	3	0	0	4	5
	8	0	15	0	4
	1	0	0	0	3
	2	0	0	1	0
	0	1	20	12	4
Afternoon	0	6	3	0	0
	0	3	0	0	4
	0	0	0	2	0
	5	8	0	0	0
	8	0	17	7	8
	0	0	1	5	6
	0	6	2	7	0
	2	1	2	1	8
	2	2	0	0	0
	6	0	12	9	9
	9	0	0	0	0
	1	0	1	8	6
	45	60	35	0	5
	0	6	0	11	1

Data Table: Taxicab Arrival Times, continued

Time of Day	Fuchsia Cab	Punctual Taxi	Rush Street Taxi	Emergency Taxi Service	Windy City Taxi Service
Evening	0	0	1	0	0
	0	0	1	0	6
	3	0	1	7	0
	2	6	0	0	7
	0	8	0	6	0
	1	0	18	1	3
	2	0	0	9	2
	1	0	0	1	0
	0	7	0	14	4
	0	0	0	0	8
	0	2	2	1	7

Times reported are in minutes and they reflect the time that the requested taxi-cab arrived relative to the time the dispatcher said it would arrive. For example, if Dave was told that the taxi would arrive in 10 minutes and the taxi actually arrived in 20 minutes, then the taxi was 10 minutes late and the number 10 is recorded in the chart. If a taxi was requested for a 7:30 pickup and it arrived right at 7:30, then a 0 is recorded because it was perfectly on time.

Problem Statement

Dave Heder is quite excited about his new job as a copilot on an international jumbo jet. He still has several concerns, though, such as how to get to the airport. Assuming that he leaves early enough for work, Dave will simply take the elevated train (known as the "L") from downtown to Midway International Airport, which is on the southwest side of town. However, when Dave's schedule does not enable him to take the train, he will need to take a taxi to work. Consequently, Dave would like to identify the most reliable taxicab company in Chicago so that he can get to the airport regularly on time.

Using the data provided, help Dave identify the taxicab company that is most likely to pick him up on time. Note that Dave has flights that leave at all times of the day (some in the morning, some in the afternoon, and some in the evening). After you identify the taxicab company with the greatest likelihood of picking him up on time, help Dave create a system that he can use to evaluate these and other taxicab companies. In a letter, explain your system to Dave so that he can use it as a guide to select companies in the future.

Chapter 4

Variability

The Zoo Problem

Visiting the zoo is an activity that interests many people. Seeing rare animals is something that we do not get to do every day, so no matter how many times one sees an elephant, giraffe, or exotic big cat, it is typically engaging. Visitors, however, seldom realize the amount of time, money, and effort that is invested in operating a zoo. This problem presents students with some of the concerns involved with running a zoo—specifically, the animals' consumption of food.

The issue of the consistency of animals' diets in the wild versus the amount of food they are fed and eat in captivity is probably not something that most people think about. It will almost certainly interest students, however, as most kids enjoy thinking about animals (exotic ones especially). This problem will hopefully get them to think about some of the subtle issues that come with keeping animals in captivity. Of course, the problem also will get them to think about statistics—and the issue of variability in particular—as it presents another practical (if somewhat unusual) opportunity for statistical analysis.

As with all MEAs, The Zoo Problem has many paths to a successful solution. Consequently, it should lend itself to some interesting discussion during the debriefing process at the conclusion of the problem.

Subject Focus of the Chapter

The statistical focus of The Zoo Problem is variability, highlighted in the problem statement with the specific line: "Principally, she would like to find

DOI: 10.4324/9781003238201-5

out which animals have the most consistent diets." By asking students to find the "most consistent" diets, they are implicitly asked to seek the least variability in the data set. The data set does not contain data from only one type of animal, however—that is to say, the weight of each animal and therefore the amount of food consumed by each animal is not consistent from animal to animal. This is something that students should consider when solving this problem.

It is important to note that some similarities exist between this and The Taxicab Problem data sets, but each problem has a different focus. The Taxicab Problem focuses on measures of central tendency and The Zoo Problem has a focus on variability. Given similar data sets, it may be comfortable to engage in precisely the same statistical procedures from problem to problem. However, implementing precisely the same procedures will not yield an adequately detailed description. In short, using precisely the same mathematical model will result in an insufficient response for one of the two problems given their different foci. The wording in The Taxicab Problem asked solvers to identify the taxicab company that was "most likely to pick him up on time." The structure of that problem statement demanded that students not necessarily seek the most consistent taxicab—which may consistently arrive 20 minutes late—but rather that they identify the one most likely to arrive promptly. The Taxicab Problem somewhat naturally lent itself to measures of central tendency more than it did to ranges.

Variability in data is a closely related topic to spread of data. Like spread of data, variability in data is often analyzed with procedures including measures of central tendency, range, and standard deviation. In this respect, Chapters 2–4 are intricately intertwined. Variability in data differs from spread of data in the respect that it is a fine-grained look at the variation in the data. Statisticians may pose the questions, "Are the data consistent throughout, or does it have some particular points that attract statisticians' attention?" and "Are data lumped in one section or another (as test scores may be), or are the data evenly spread?" Topics used to gain further understanding of variability are standard deviation, interquartile range, sum of squares, and variance, but an intimate understanding of the aforementioned topics is not necessary to be successful in understanding variability with The Zoo Problem.

Links to NCTM Content Standards

Similarities also exist between the content standards met by The Zoo Problem and those met by The Taxicab Problem. This is the case because some standards have more than one benchmark or expectation in them. For example, the expectation "Find, use, and interpret measures of center and spread, including mean, median, and interquartile range" has applications to each problem, although each mathematical concept is ideally not used in each problem. As previously mentioned, many authentic mathematical problems (Chamberlin, 2011) have more than one solution process. This further complicates the issue of guaranteeing that one problem will specifically meet one or more standards. As with The Taxicab Problem, one group may create one mathematical model and another group may create another mathematical problem. Hence, the standards listed are those that will likely be used by various groups. Highly open-ended problems, as these MEAs are, coupled with students working in groups to solve the problems, create an issue regarding which standards are met by all students. The only way to ensure that NCTM content standards are covered is to have a teacher-centered classroom. MEAs are highly student-centered problems while the problem-solving process is taking place, but the teacher can review concepts during the debriefing process that serve to highlight various approaches and therefore meet various standards.

For The Zoo Problem, nearly all students will meet the following NCTM content standards:

- Find, use, and interpret measures of center and spread, including mean, median, and interquartile range (grade band 6–8).
- Discuss and understand the correspondence between data sets and their graphical representations, especially histograms, stem-and-leaf plots, box plots, and scatterplots (grade band 6–8).
- Use observations about differences between two or more samples to make conjectures about the populations from which the samples were taken (grade band 6–8).
- Identify trends in bivariate data and find functions that model the data or transform the data so that they can be modeled (grade band 9–12).
- Understand how sample statistics reflect the values of population parameters and use sampling distributions as the basis for informal inference (grade band 9–12).

The following content standards may be covered by some, but not all, problem solvers:

- Select, create, and use appropriate graphical representations of data, including histograms, box plots, and scatterplots (grade band 6–8).
- Make conjectures about possible relationships between two characteristics of a sample on the basis of scatterplots of the data and approximate lines of fit (grade band 6–8).
- Understand histograms, parallel box plots, and scatterplots and use them to display data (grade band 9–12).

- Use simulations to explore the variability of sample statistics from a known population and to construct sampling distributions (grade band 9–12).
- For univariate measurement data, be able to display the distribution, describe its shape, and select and calculate summary statistics (grade band 9–12). *Note:* Technically this is bivariate data, but as problem solvers are analyzing singular data sets and not comparing the respective data sets to other data sets, the term univariate data applies.

Naturally, the extent to which these expectations are covered is contingent upon whether or not problem solvers create scatterplots to respond to the problem and/or whether or not the scatterplot is a component of their mathematical model. In addition, for all MEAs in this book, the algebra standard "Model and solve contextualized problems using various representations, such as graphs, tables, and equations" is met.

Questions to Pose to Students

Needless to say, instructors need to be prepared with questions prior to implementing the activity. Solving the problem in as many ways as possible will help instructors prepare questions and it will also help them generate questions on the spot. Some questions that are likely to arise specific to this problem include:

- What mathematical processes do the terms *consistent diet* or *consistency* evoke in your mind?
- Would considering any measures of central tendency help you in finding how consistent the data sets are?
- In your model, have you considered the fact that there are widely different amounts of food consumed by most of the animals (data sets)?
- What does the standard deviation actually indicate in this problem?
- Have you considered using more than one measure (e.g., measure of spread or central tendency) to create your mathematical model?
- In considering the several models that you've proposed, which one seems to provide the most detailed analysis of the data sets?
- Do outliers exist in any of the data sets and, if so, what if any impact did this have on your data analysis?
- Would the creation of a table or graph help you organize your data more efficiently than you currently have it organized?
- Does the size of the animal have any bearing on how much food it consumes?

The Zoo Problem

58   STATISTICS FOR KIDS

Potential Student Responses

As with all problems in this book, student responses can be quite varied and are contingent upon at least three factors. First, the connection that students make with the context can greatly impact their final products. Second, their understanding and innate ability to comprehend the concept of variability prior to being introduced to the concept will impact their products. Finally, the representations that groups choose to utilize will provide a great deal of insight into the mathematical models created. That said, the following are some solutions students are most likely to come up with.

Solution 1

Range, a measure of spread, is the most common approach that students use when tackling The Zoo Problem. This approach is not completely flawed, but it does have one serious caveat: Using the range may be a questionable approach if the students do not account for the various ranges for respective animals (this problem may be endemic throughout all mathematical models created to solve this problem). In other words, it is not appropriate to compare the range of food consumed by the elephant to the range of food consumed by the ring-tailed lemur because the two animals consume radically different amounts of food.

The typical problem solver, even in grades 4–6, should be able to realize that simply analyzing the range of food consumed per animal is not a fair statistical comparison. If a group of problem solvers did compare the two ranges, it would quickly become apparent that the elephant has the largest range of food consumed, at 54 pounds of food per day, and that the ring-tailed lemur has the smallest range, at 0.44 pounds of food per day.

	Jaguar	Zebra	Ring-Tailed Lemur	Elephant	Red Wolf
Range	4.2	6.4	0.44	54	3.6
Mean	4.35	20.02667	1.994138	324.98	3.506667
Median	4.45	20.15	2.03	327.8	3.5

The two ranges can only adequately be compared if a control mechanism is used. An example of a control mechanism for this problem might be to look, first, at the average amount of food consumed by the elephant, which is 324.98 pounds per day (arithmetic mean) or 327.8 pounds per day (median). It could therefore be considered appropriate to say that the elephant consumes approximately 325 pounds of food per day. In comparison, the ring-tailed lemur only consumes 1.99 pounds of food per day (arithmetic mean) or 2.03 pounds of food per day (median). It would therefore be safe to state that the ring-tailed lemur consumes approximately 2 pounds of food per day. By comparing the average amount of food consumed per day to the value of the range for each animal, students can attempt to formulate a means of accounting for the large variation in ranges between animals.

Solution 2

One way of looking at the range is to plot the data, for instance, as a scatterplot or a histogram (although the scatterplot is likely to be more informative than the histogram), and to compare the ranges. This is simply another version of analyzing the range. There are two caveats with this approach. First, the same problem explicated in Solution 1 is evident again here: That is to say, the varied differences in ranges need to be controlled for in some manner. A tool that can account for the differences in amount of food consumed per day should ideally be applied to compare a really large animal (elephant), a moderately large animal (zebra), two animals of somewhat similar size (jaguar and red wolf), and a fairly small animal (ring-tailed lemur).

Outliers can also dramatically impact conclusions reached in Solutions 1 and 2. Plotting a graph may help make outliers more visible to students, and can help them appropriately account for this problem. (For more information on outliers, see the Outliers section immediately following the Potential Student Responses section in Chapter 3.)

Instructors should also note that simply creating a scatterplot or a histogram is not considered to be a comprehensive mathematical model in itself, but it can provide great insight with respect to the final model created.

Solution 3

Another approach to solve the problem is to draw an approximate line of best fit from the scatterplot or to use the arithmetic mean for each animal if the pictorial representation is not desired and to use the line of best fit or the arithmetic mean to identify the absolute value for each data point. Once this is done, a composite or sum can be calculated relative to the line of best fit or the arithmetic mean. Some problem solvers will not realize that this mathematical model should theoretically result in a composite or sum of zero if the line is drawn accurately. As a result, this is an example of a flawed mathematical model. It is important to note that with multiple iterations flawed mathematical models often result, with substantial persistency, in the creation of refined mathematical models that often provide some insight to the problem solvers. An interesting issue with this model, flawed as it may be, is that this approach

The Zoo Problem

does control for the wide variety of ranges (spread) in food consumed by animals with widely disparate diets.

Solution 4

If students have been taught how to use standard deviation (and it is suggested that they be introduced to the procedure upon completion of the MEA in Chapter 3), they may realize that the problem statement and the data sets in this problem lend themselves to its use. A noticeable caveat with using the SD is that many students in grades 4–6 often have trouble understanding what the SD actually tells the problem solvers. As a result, they may simply look at the final SD statistics and select the lowest one as having the lowest range/spread and therefore as having the greatest consistency. The respective SD figures for the animals are presented in the following table.

	Jaguar	Zebra	Ring-Tailed Lemur	Elephant	Red Wolf
Standard Deviation	0.8135703	1.5440505	0.1051366	12.135965	0.8419736

Unfortunately, the SD suffers from the same problem that most other mathematical models do with this problem: That is to say, one cannot simply look at the SD of the ring-tailed lemur and select it given the fact that it has the lowest SD. This is because, again, the ranges of food consumed differ greatly from animal to animal.

A statistical procedure known as the F-Test can be applied to the data sets to see which animal really has the lowest SD. It is important to note, however, that problem solvers in grades 4–6 cannot reasonably be expected to know what an F-Test is, nor should they be expected to apply it to this problem and the subsequent mathematical model created. In the case that students decide to use the SD, the instructor should be aware that an F-Test needs to be done when comparing more than one SD. This is something that could possibly be introduced to students during the debriefing period, but it is only recommended for students of extremely advanced statistical capabilities. (Please note that instruction regarding how to perform an F-Test lies beyond the scope of this book. Information can be found online regarding how to use it, and teachers are encouraged to research the topic if further information is needed or desired.)

Solution 5

Another approach to solving The Zoo Problem is to create an Interquartile Range (IQR) or a semi-IQR. To compute the IQR, simply arrange all data from lowest to highest and identify the midpoint (median) of the data set. In this problem, the median of the jaguar, zebra, elephant, and red wolf data sets are the precise points between data points 15 and 16. If the two points are the same, then this number is used; if they vary, then they are added together and divided by two. Given the fact that one data point is missing from the ring-tailed lemur data set, that median is precisely 15. The respective medians for each animal are shown in the following table.

	Jaguar	Zebra	Ring-Tailed Lemur	Elephant	Red Wolf
Q1	4.0	19	1.9	312.7	2.8
Q2 (median)	4.4	19.9	2.005	326.4	3.4
Q3	4.8	21	2.06	331.9	4.1
IQR	0.8	2	0.16	19.2	1.3
Semi-IQR	0.4	1	0.08	9.6	0.65

To compute the first quartile (Q1) and the third quartile (Q3), one simply finds the medians on either side of the currently split data sets. At this point, the median of the overall sets (Q2) and the medians of each subset (Q1 and Q3) have been identified. To find the IQR, a problem solver simply subtracts Q1 from Q3.

To compute a semi-IQR, one computes the IQR and then divides all numbers in half. This gives the appearance that the statistics are not as dramatically different as they appear to be when, in fact, dividing all final IQR statistics by two simply changes the factor of the IQR by two. (Note that the IQR and semi-IQR data align perfectly with the standard deviation data. This is to be expected, and is a direct result of the large and small ranges in food due to the amount consumed on a daily basis by respective animals.)

As with the previous approaches, instructors should be aware that, in order to account for the varied ranges in the data, a control mechanism should ideally be applied.

Solution 6

A final solution offered, and perhaps the most comprehensive solution, is to identify the median for each animal and to compute the absolute value of all deviations from the median in an attempt to see what percentage variation exists from animal to animal. This solution can be elucidated with an example.

Given the data for the jaguar, the median is 4.45. Using the proposed model, a problem solver would look at all individual data points to compute the absolute value difference in sum: That is to say, one would identify all of the differences from individual data points and add them to create a composite (or sum). For the jaguar, using the model, the composite would be 17.1 pounds. This figure can then be looked at relative to the median of 4.45. The composite number can be viewed as a percentage of the median or it can be viewed as a factor of 4.45; either term is appropriate (the decision on which one is used is simply a debate of semantics). The final composite of 17.1 is a factor of 3.84 or 384% higher than the median. The same approach can be executed with all other data sets (i.e., the zebra, ring-tailed lemur, elephant, and red wolf). This controls for the variation in the amount of food consumed by all animals. Therefore, students are able to compare the widely different diets between the animals in an appropriate fashion.

Notes on Implementation

There are several considerations to keep in mind when implementing The Zoo Problem. First, from an assessment perspective, it is suggested that a scatterplot or a histogram not suffice as a stand-alone mathematical model. Pictorial representations such as analyzing skew(ness) or kurtosis of the data set can aid in understanding the distribution and range of the data, but using graphs to interpret data does not constitute a mathematical model. These approaches should not be discouraged, however, because they can provide great insight regarding how the data are behaving. In addition, such pictorial representations may give ideas as to how a mathematical model can be created.

This comment has been made repeatedly throughout the chapter (and the data set was intentionally made as it was to present this problem), but it bears stressing that students and the facilitator seriously consider the variation in amount of food consumed. All data sets in the overall data set are not directly comparable. This is because the elephant eats a large amount of food on a daily basis, and the other animals consume far less food. Consequently, it would be logical to assume that the elephant would possess the largest range of food consumed. Still, this statistic does not answer the question posed regarding which animal has the most consistent (or least variable) diet. Some mathematical models will not consider this issue, whereas other, more sophisticated mathematical models would have some control mechanism to account for this difference. The most sophisticated approach would include something such as an F-Test when analyzing the SD of the data sets. Again, however, it should not be expected that students be familiar with this process at this age.

Of the solutions provided, only Solution 6 enables problem solvers to accurately compare the various animals, given the wide variety of diets; this is because it uses the median and variation is measured as a factor of the median. The debriefing period should be used to point this process out to students, if they do not come up with it on their own.

A general knowledge of the size of the animals is not a prerequisite to solving The Zoo Problem, but it could be helpful. Moreover, at the heart of this problem is the notion that some animals (e.g., the wolf and jaguar), even when in a controlled environment such as the zoo, may still behave in a feast or famine fashion because that is their very nature. Others, such as the ring-tailed lemur, may adapt quite nicely to zoo life and have the cognitive ability to realize that a consistent food source will be placed in the pen or cage each day, thus alleviating food anxiety or the desire to eat vast amounts of food at any one sitting. Still another consideration, not mentioned in this problem, is how long each animal had been at the zoo. If, for instance, the elephant had been conditioned to a constant food source, its diet may be more consistent than a new elephant's diet.

All of these conversations have to deal with the concept of making inferences from presented data sets. It may be asserted that learning relatively basic statistical concepts is at the heart, or is the purpose, of statistics, as doing so allows statisticians to make inferences from data sets. The main reason for engaging in these MEAs, which consist of mostly descriptive statistical procedures, is to give aspiring statisticians an increased likelihood of success with inferential statistical procedures in the future.

The Zoo Problem

Suzanne Reimenshneider has quite an interest in animals, and one day she would like to become a veterinarian. After several visits to the Potawatomi Zoo, she asked her parents if the zoo might have a job for her. Given her young age, Suzanne offered to volunteer until she was old enough to legally work. After going to the zoo to inquire about volunteer opportunities, Suzanne's mother learned that she knew the director of the zoo. They met with the director, and Suzanne told him that she wanted to work there. Within the week, Suzanne had a job cleaning pens, feeding animals, and working at the information booth at the zoo.

Since starting work, Suzanne has developed many interests and concerns about the animals. For instance, she has many questions concerning the health care of the animals. She also is interested in knowing how the director finds animals to inhabit the zoo, and she is interested in the diets of the animals. Specifically, she is curious about what types of food the animals eat and how closely the diets align with what they would actually eat in the wild. She met with the zoo director to find the answers to these questions.

One question that the zoo director was not able to answer related to the consistency of the volume of food in the animals' diets. Some animals, domestic or wild, are known for eating as much as they can. Cows, for instance, are rumored to eat whatever is in front of them, as long as food is there. Other animals, such as cats, will typically eat only when hungry. There are many factors that influence hunger and the amount of food that a domestic or wild animal will eat. Upon talking with the zoo director, Suzanne decided to collect some data on the amount of food that several animals consume each day. The only instrument that she has for data collection is a scale that she uses to measure the animals' food each day. As she is not at the zoo for each feeding, she has enlisted the help of a friend who works in the mornings. After carefully measuring the amount of food and placing it in the appropriate food trough, she will have her friend weigh the food in the morning, and then she will monitor the difference.

Readiness Questions

1. Why does Suzanne have an interest in the zoo?

2. How did Suzanne get a job at the zoo?

3. Do you think all animals eat a consistent amount of food each day? Why or why not?

4. Other than finding the weight of the food, is there a way to measure how much food the animals consistently eat each day?

5. What does consistency mean to you?

Data Table: Food Consumption by Animals

Day	Jaguar	Zebra	Ring-Tailed Lemur	Elephant	Red Wolf
1	4.7	20.3	1.82	328.9	2.4
2	4.6	19.8	1.79	331.7	3.6
3	4.5	21	2.01	308.4	3.8
4	1.8	20.7	1.89	297.5	4.1
5	5.2	20.7	2.05	311.1	2.8
6	4.8	20.5	1.93	328.5	4.4
7	5.3	17.3	2.00	331.8	2.9
8	4.6	16.5	2.20	317.5	3.1
9	4.4	18.7	2.15	309.8	3.3
10	3.8	16.8	2.04	312.7	3.7
11	4.1	18.5	1.97	328.5	2.9
12	6.0	20.0	2.06	317.6	3.5
13	3.2	20.5	1.92	327.1	3.3
14	3.4	21.7	1.88	324.3	2.7
15	2.8	21.0	1.76	317.6	3.2
16	4.7	19.5	Not Available	351.5	4.1
17	4.1	22.9	2.04	330.6	2.7
18	4.3	19.0	2.07	325.7	3.9
19	4.1	21.0	1.99	310.8	3.5
20	5.1	22.1	2.11	341.2	4.5
21	5.2	19.2	2.07	329.3	2.1
22	4.8	19.5	2.03	333.7	1.9
23	4.5	19.5	2.06	334.2	5.5
24	5.0	19.0	2.10	338.5	4.7
25	3.8	22.0	2.05	321.6	3.2
26	4.1	21.2	1.91	331.9	3.9
27	4.0	19.4	2.05	322.4	4.3
28	4.4	22.0	1.88	306.7	3.9
29	4.4	21.2	1.97	338.2	2.5
30	4.8	19.3	2.03	340.1	4.8

All weight is presented in pounds. It is important to be aware that, because animals' diets are highly controlled at the zoo, these data may be somewhat misleading. Also, different animals may vary their eating habits at different times of the year, so some may seem to have greater fluctuations than they might have otherwise.

Problem Statement

Suzanne has been extremely careful in collecting the data about the animals at the zoo. She was so particular about the accuracy of the data collection process that she held a short meeting with several of the workers to show them precisely how she wanted the data collected. To measure the amount of food consumed, data collectors have been asked to weigh the food before they give it to the animals and then, 2 hours after the food is delivered, the food is picked up and weighed a second time. The number recorded in the data table reflects the amount of food consumed by the animal; the values were determined by subtracting the end weight of the food from the beginning weight of the food. For example, if on Day 1 the jaguar was given 7.0 pounds of food and after 2 hours 2.3 pounds of food remained, then the jaguar consumed 4.7 pounds of food, which is the piece of data recorded in the first box in the data table. At this point, Suzanne has a very accurate set of data. Now, she is faced with how to do the data analysis.

Principally, she would like to find out which animals have the most consistent diets. To do this, she needs to come up with some way to measure consistency and to be able to rank order the animals from most to least consistent eaters. Help Suzanne find a way to measure the consistency of the volume of food eaten by each animal, and pay close attention to your process so that you can document your approach. She would like to use the method created with additional animals at the zoo so that she can do an analysis of all of the animals in future months.

Chapter 5

Correlation

The Stock Market Problem

With each day comes a new experience in the stock market. Investors and brokers can gain or lose thousands or even millions of dollars in mere hours. These dramatic changes come about as a result of even modest changes in the market. The stock market can be a fairly delicate mechanism. It serves as a barometer for the economy as a whole.

In The Stock Market Problem, students are presented with a familiar situation in the business world: following and understanding the movement of stocks, so as to make informed decisions that result in financial reward. In this problem, solvers are given data from three indices in the U.S.: the Dow Jones Industrial Average (the Dow), the Nasdaq Composite, and the Standard & Poor's 500 (S&P 500). Students are asked to identify whether or not there is any relationship between the three indices and, if so, they are asked to identify quantitatively and/or qualitatively what the relationship is.

Students at this age may not be familiar with what stocks are, so it is important to explain the concept to them and make sure that they fully understand it before starting work on the problem. They should be able to grasp its nature rather easily, as they will be familiar with the importance of making money and the need for companies to make money in order to grow. What they may not understand is that people give companies this money, and that they do so with the hope of achieving their own financial reward (hence, the nature of the stock market). Although students' success in solving this problem does not necessarily depend upon understanding this relationship, it is always important to give as much contextual information as possible when implementing MEAs.

DOI: 10.4324/9781003238201-6

Subject Focus of the Chapter

The Stock Market Problem was designed specifically to enable students the opportunity to investigate the statistical concept of correlation. It is hoped that problem solvers will create mathematical models that may not mimic the correlation process perfectly, but that help provide insight into how an actual correlation works. A correlation is simply a statistical process that indicates whether or not a relationship exists between two or more variables. The term *correlation*, however, should be avoided at all costs; facilitators should use the term *relationship* rather than correlation as the problem is implemented.

Central to this problem is the notion that two data sets may be related—or, as the appropriate statistical term suggests, the two data sets may be co-related (hence the term *correlation*: co + relation). The prefix *co* of course suggests two items, entities, or facets intermingling, as is the case with terms such as cooperate, copilot, codependent, and coworker. Correlation indicates that one set of data is looked at in relation to another set of data. Statisticians are known to pose questions such as, "How did the two sets of data correlate?" or "How did one (set of data) behave relative to another one (set of data)?"

The statistical process of correlation is often used in everyday life in formal and informal situations, and it is a concept on which many other far more complicated statistical procedures (such as structural equations modeling and exploratory and confirmatory factor analysis) are based. As such, the statistical concept of correlation is imperative to understanding higher level statistical procedures.

Links to NCTM Content Standards

The central focus of this problem deals with determining what, if any, relationship exists between the three different stock markets. To that end, the following NCTM content standards will typically be met:

- Discuss and understand the correspondence between data sets and their graphical representations, especially histograms, stem-and-leaf plots, box plots, and scatterplots (grade band 6–8).
- Use observations about differences between two or more samples to make conjectures about the populations from which the samples were taken (grade band 6–8).
- Make conjectures about possible relationships between two characteristics of a sample on the basis of scatterplots of the data and approximate lines of fit (grade band 6–8).

- For bivariate measurement data, be able to display a scatterplot, describe its shape, and determine regression coefficients, regression equations, and correlation coefficients using technological tools (grade band 9–12).
- Identify trends in bivariate data and find functions that model the data or transform the data so that they can be modeled (grade band 9–12).

The following content standards may be covered by some, but not all problem solvers:
- Select, create, and use appropriate graphical representations of data, including histograms, box plots, and scatterplots (grade band 6–8).
- Understand histograms, parallel box plots, and scatterplots and use them to display data (grade band 9–12).

Finally, as for all MEAs in this book, the algebra standard "Model and solve contextualized problems using various representations, such as graphs, tables, and equations" is met.

Questions to Pose to Students

This MEA is a quintessential example of a problem that requires a good deal of forethought and some playing with the data sets prior to implementation. It is necessary to realize that simply administering this problem, or any other MEA of sufficient complexity, without a good deal of familiarity prior to implementation will often result in a less than successful learning experience and a weaker exploration of statistical concepts.

The instructor should ask several questions during the implementation of this MEA. Some examples are as follows:
- Is it necessary to look at the two data sets and to control for variations in the markets by reasoning proportionally in an attempt to make the two data sets of similar proportion?
- Without doing any computations or calculations, do you notice any patterns in the data sets?
- When you think of the term *relationship*, what comes to mind?
- What procedures do you have in place to identify a relationship?
- You may be familiar with what a correlation is, but is there any method of roughly estimating a relationship, or correlation, without doing any computations?

- Do you think it matters if you rearrange the data points in a set or do all individual data points need to be kept in the order in which they appear in the data set?
- Can you make any observations about any one data set (the Dow, Nasdaq Composite, or S&P 500) without looking at the other two sets?
- Do any data sets appear to be predictors for any other data sets?

Potential Student Responses

Many individuals know vaguely what a correlation is, but they may not be able to compute one. This should be the case with students of advanced intellect in grades 4–6. Few, if any, will actually know how to compute a correlation coefficient (i.e., the number that tells what the correlation is), but most should be able to grasp whether or not any relationship exists. Problem solvers working on The Stock Market Problem are asked to identify whether or not any of the markets are related to each other and then to create a mathematical model to explain their solution.

Solution 1

Perhaps the most apparent solution to The Stock Market Problem is to look for a percentage change in the respective data sets to see if deviation exists. This is an informal means of measuring the relationship (or correlation) of two data sets. As an example, one could analyze individual data sets relative to one another (i.e., A:B, B:C, and C:A). The lower the deviation between two sets, the better the relationship. The larger the deviation between the two sets, the worse the relationship is. One caveat, however, is that the positive changes (gains) and the negative changes (losses) need to be considered. So, for instance, if one market gained one day and the other market lost by a similar amount on the same day, the two would be considered to have an inverse, or negative, relationship, rather than a positive relationship.

A second note is that problem solvers may encounter an issue similar to the one they experienced in The Zoo Problem in Chapter 4, if the variation in market values is not considered. This is because the Nasdaq Composite is typically about 2–2.5 times higher than the S&P 500, and the Dow is about 4.5–5 times higher than the Nasdaq Composite, thus making the Dow about 9–12.5 times higher than the S&P 500. Hence, it is problematic to simply compare one market to another without any concern for control from market to market.

One easy trick that experts in the business world use to control for variation from market to market is to simply calculate a percentage change, positive or negative, for each market. As an example, the percentage change from a market that opens the day at 9,000 and ends the day at 9,250—a fairly healthy gain for the day—is approximately +2.8%. There are several processes to calculate the percentage change, and the most common method used to find the difference in the two numbers (i.e., +250 points) is to ascertain the amount of change and divide it by the initial or starting figure. In this case, the +250 would be divided into (+) 9,000 to attain the ultimate result of approximately +2.8%. If this were the percentage change for Day 1 for a market, this data point could be compared to the percentage change of another market to seek the difference as an absolute value. For instance, if the change on the same day in another market was -0.65%, then the problem solver could look at the two data points relative to one another (+2.8% and -0.65%) to identify the one that had the most significant gain or loss.

Something for problem solvers to consider is that for a strong correlation, when one market gains, the other should also gain consistently. Similarly, when one loses, the other should lose consistently as well. If one market gains and the other market loses, or vice-versa, then this hampers the correlation coefficient, as the markets are not consistent with one another.

Finally, the amount of the percentage gain or loss will impact the relationship (correlation coefficient) a great deal. That is to say, a loss of 0.5% in one market and a raise of 1.1% in another market will not hurt the correlation to the same extent that a loss of 7.25% in one market and a raise of 5.125% in another market would. Remember, there are several ways to compute the change each day, but the percentage change for each market is likely the most simplistic and logical approach because it enables the solver to control for varying values of markets.

Solution 2

Another mathematical model that might suffice to solve The Stock Market Problem is some version of a scatterplot. As stated in Chapter 4, a pictorial representation should not suffice as a stand-alone mathematical model. However, a pictorial representation such as a scatterplot might help problem solvers compare data from day to day somewhat readily. From a scatterplot, a line of best fit can ideally be drawn to provide insight regarding the relationship from one set to another. Provided on the next page are three sample data sets and scatterplots intended to show a very strong correlation (i.e., $r = 1.0$), a somewhat moderate correlation, and an inverse correlation (i.e., $r = -1.0$).

Data Set 1: AZ	
A	Z
1	1
2	2
3	3
4	4
5	5
6	6
7	7
8	8
9	9
10	10
$r = 1.0$ $r^2 = 1.0$	

Data Set 2: BY	
B	Y
1	7
10	3
2	5
9	1
3	4
8	6
4	7
7	2
5	5
6	10
$r = -.4403855$ $r^2 = .1939394$	

Data Set 3: CX	
C	X
1	10
2	9
3	8
4	7
5	6
6	5
7	4
8	3
9	2
10	1
$r = -1.0$ $r^2 = 1.0$	

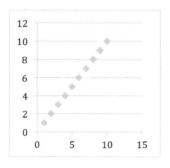 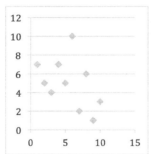 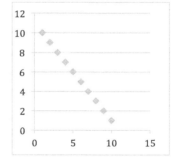

r^2 indicates correlation; it ranges from 0.0 to 1.0, 0.0 indicating no correlation and 1.0 indicating a perfect correlation. This statistic can be used to help problem solvers identify the strength of the relationship.

Note that, although it is beyond the scope of this book (and beyond reasonable expectations of a student's knowledge at this age) to explain how to formulate the correlation coefficient (r), students do not need to be able to calculate r to understand the concept at hand. Depending on their ability, however, teachers may want to introduce the procedure during the debriefing period following the activity.

With ample discussion of the intricacies of the scatterplots, this mathematical model may be accepted contingent upon the facilitator's discretion.

Solution 3

Yet another pictorial approach that could be used to create a mathematical model is to create a histogram of respective data sets and to then place the respective histograms on top of each other to seek similarity in the two data sets. The main issue with this approach is that the histograms would need to have some mechanism to control for the rather disparate data from set to set, due to the wide variation in the market values. For example, it would be problematic to compare the Dow data (which is in the 9,000 to 10,000 range) with the S&P 500 data (which is in the 900 to 1,000 range). Hence, some control mechanism must be used to enable problem solvers the opportunity to compare relatively different data sets. An example of a control mechanism that students this age might be able to create would be to norm or place on a scale all of the data. For instance, one way to compare data across indices would be to place them on a scale of 100 (i.e., using a percentage). In doing this, students could compare indices with rather large numbers (the Dow) and small numbers (the S&P 500).

Solution 4

A more advanced approach to The Stock Market Problem would reflect an awareness that the data sets can be compared without using a control mechanism. This is because, to compute a correlation, two data sets do not need to be normalized, or made to have the same measure or standard, to be compared (Weida, 1927). If proportionality exists from set to set (i.e., each is gaining or losing consistently with one another), then a fairly rudimentary relationship can be estimated. In fact, one very basic idea is to simply identify whether a gain or a loss occurred on each day and to compare that data with data in the other sets. In this case, a problem solver could have three sets of data with nothing more than a simple plus (+) or minus (-) to indicate a gain or loss for each day. Students could then seek the percentage of days on which agreement occurred (i.e., a gain matched a gain or a loss was linked with a loss) and create a rough estimate of a relationship. If, for instance the gains and losses linked with one another on 80% of the days, then perhaps the problem solvers could look at the relationship as being approximately 80%. This model is not nearly as sophisticated as a formal correlation, but it does enable problem solvers the chance to see what level of harmony exists between two data sets.

Notes on Implementation

The postactivity discussion is a good time to introduce your students to the formal term *correlation* and its definition. It might be helpful to discuss what a correlation is by showing at least three data sets, as provided in Solution 2. If desired, a facilitator could also discuss how/why the range can be viewed as ranging from -1.0 to 1.0 (the correlation coefficient, or *r*) or the more familiar 0 to 1.0, which is achieved by squaring the correlation coefficient (r^2). A scatterplot could be helpful in illustrating this. In any event, a perfect 1.0 or a perfect -1.0 *r* value (both when squared create an r^2 value of 1.0) are the strongest correlation coefficients and are therefore quite informative. Unfortunately, each of these values has been referred to as a correlation coefficient in statistics textbooks, which makes understanding the concept of correlation increasingly difficult for early learners of statistical concepts.

If the problem looks too difficult for students, the instructor should consider removing one of the markets and simply ask students for one relationship (market A:B) rather than three relationships (markets A:B, B:C, and C:A). If desired, the instructor could also discuss what constitutes weak, moderate, and strong relationships. Although the exact definitions are somewhat debated, it is generally accepted by most statisticians that if relationships, or correlation coefficients, are broken into three strata ranging from 0 to 1.0—e.g., 0.0 to .33 (weak), .34 to .66 (moderate), and .67 to 1.0 (strong)—then three categories (weak, moderate, and strong; also referred to as low, moderate, and high) exist. Some statisticians prefer a slightly more stringent standard, such as 0.0 to .4 (weak), .41 to .69 (moderate), and .7 to 1.0 (strong).

It is important for students to understand that realizing a very nominal relationship exists is sometimes as important as realizing that a strong relationship exists. A weak correlation is not completely useless because realizing that a very weak correlation exists can be informative: It reveals little relationship in the two data sets. Sometimes, the realization that a poor correlation exists is very helpful to statisticians. Further, a mistake that many novice statisticians commit is to say that "no correlation" exists. Technically, this is really never true unless one ends up with a correlation of 0.0, but even this is flawed terminology. Saying that no correlation exists is similar to saying that no temperature exists when the temperature is 0° F. There is not an absence of a temperature or an absence of correlation: There is simply a 0.0 correlation. Even with a correlation of .01, one should say that a very weak correlation exists because, by definition, that is true. Problem solvers could also realize that an inverse relationship, or inverse correlation (such as a negative one), is evident, but that information is not directly solicited in this problem. Generally speaking, students are simply asked to identify if any such relationship can be identified between the indices.

Students should be careful not to line up the data from highest change to lowest change or vice-versa because this will inherently increase the correlation coefficient by giving the appearance that all data was increased or decreased consistently on respective days. This is therefore misleading and a somewhat commonly committed error when looking at a relationship.

Finally, students and facilitators should remember that a relationship may exist between two of the markets (e.g., A:B and B:C, or B:C and C:A), but not all three markets.

The Stock Market Problem

The stock market is an important facet of the economy. It allows people to give money to businesses in exchange for stock, or tiny pieces of ownership of a company. People can buy stock in all sorts of companies. When a company does well and makes a profit, its stock prices often go up and the people who own stock in that company make money. When a business does poorly, however, stockholders can lose some or all of their investment.

Although it is referred to as a "market" (like a supermarket), this is actually a bit of a misnomer. It is not a place that you can visit, and there are no products. The term *stock market* simply refers to the organized trading of stocks, which is facilitated by organizations known as stock exchanges. Stock exchanges provide central locations to record and keep track of the trading activity. There are many stock exchanges, such as the New York Stock Exchange, the world's largest.

Market indices track the performance of different companies' stock. The Nikkei 225 in Japan, the NZ50 in New Zealand, the Hang Seng Index in Hong Kong, the FTSE 100 in the United Kingdom, the DAX in Germany, and the Madrid Stock Exchange General Index in Spain are leading market indices from around the world. In the U.S., the Dow Jones Industrial Average, the Nasdaq Composite, and the Standard and Poor's 500 (S&P 500) serve as the main market indices. Together, they represent the stock of most major companies throughout the country.

One of the best-known market indices, the Dow Jones Industrial Average (often referred to simply as the Dow) is comprised of 30 leading companies. It is often looked at as an indicator of the general state of the economy. Charles Dow designed this market index in 1896 to represent the business market, which at the time included industries such as sugar, leather, tobacco, gas, rubber, and coal. Today, the Dow is led by retail, oil, technology, pharmaceutical, and entertainment companies. Of the current companies, General Electric has been included the longest; it was added in 1907.

The Nasdaq Composite is an index of many of the stocks traded on the NASDAQ stock exchange. Because many new companies have elected to join the NASDAQ, the number of companies on this index has grown from 100 back in 1971 to more than 5,500 today. This index includes many companies in the technology sector, where market trends change quickly. As a result, performance of these stocks can shift rapidly.

Created in 1957 by the Standard & Poor's Corporation, the S&P 500 tracks the top 500 publicly traded companies in the U.S. Industries such as transportation, utilities, financial services, technology, health care, energy, communications, services, capital goods, basic materials, and consumer products are represented. Many consider it the most accurate reflection of the U.S. stock market today. This high regard has led many money managers and pension plan administrators to use it as a benchmark for judging the overall performance of their funds.

Readiness Questions

1. In your own words, define the stock market.

2. Name a stock market index that is known internationally.

3. What were some of the industries originally represented by the Dow?

4. How many companies are included on the Nasdaq Composite today?

5. Which market index is considered to be the leading indicator of the U.S. stock market today?

Data Table: Stock Market Values

Date	Dow: Open	Dow: Close	Nasdaq Composite: Open	Nasdaq Composite: Close	S&P 500: Open	S&P 500: Close
			Market: Period			
October 10	11,104.64	11,433.18	2,522.72	2,566.05	1,158.15	1,194.89
October 7	11,123.41	11,103.12	2,509.61	2,479.35	1,165.03	1,155.46
October 6	10,940.03	11,123.33	2,459.05	2,506.82	1,144.11	1,164.97
October 5	10,800.39	10,939.95	2,398.37	2,460.51	1,124.03	1,144.03
October 4	10,650.31	10,808.71	2,312.68	2,404.82	1,097.42	1,123.95
October 3	10,912.02	10,655.30	2,401.19	2,335.83	1,131.21	1,099.23
September 30	11,152.32	10,913.38	2,444.77	2,415.40	1,159.93	1,131.42
September 29	11,012.79	11,153.98	2,535.52	2,480.76	1,151.74	1,160.40
September 28	11,189.10	11,010.90	2,557.86	2,491.58	1,175.39	1,151.06
September 27	11,045.38	11,190.69	2,560.78	2,546.83	1,163.32	1,175.38
September 26	10,771.86	11,043.86	2,496.98	2,516.69	1,136.91	1,162.95
September 23	10,732.77	10,771.48	2,438.63	2,483.23	1,128.82	1,136.43
September 22	11,121.89	10,733.83	2,466.06	2,455.67	1,164.55	1,129.56
September 21	11,408.58	11,124.84	2,601.06	2,538.19	1,203.63	1,166.76
September 20	11,401.39	11,408.66	2,623.89	2,590.24	1,204.50	1,202.09
September 19	11,506.67	11,401.01	2,584.35	2,612.83	1,214.99	1,204.09
September 16	11,433.48	11,509.09	2,607.12	2,622.31	1,209.21	1,216.01
September 15	11,247.64	11,433.18	2,595.45	2,607.07	1,189.44	1,209.11
September 14	11,106.83	11,246.73	2,548.45	2,572.55	1,173.32	1,188.68
September 13	11,054.99	11,105.85	2,502.59	2,532.15	1,162.59	1,172.87
September 12	10,990.01	11,061.12	2,442.86	2,495.09	1,153.50	1,162.27
September 9	11,294.53	10,992.13	2,508.12	2,467.99	1,185.37	1,154.23
September 8	11,414.64	11,295.81	2,533.81	2,529.14	1,197.98	1,185.90
September 7	11,138.01	11,414.86	2,511.50	2,548.94	1,165.85	1,198.62
September 6	11,237.23	11,139.30	2,417.61	2,473.83	1,173.97	1,165.24
September 2	11,492.06	11,240.26	2,497.28	2,480.33	1,203.90	1,173.97
September 1	11,613.30	11,493.57	2,583.34	2,546.04	1,219.12	1,204.42
August 31	11,560.55	11,613.53	2,589.75	2,579.46	1,213.00	1,218.89
August 30	11,532.06	11,559.95	2,547.07	2,576.11	1,209.76	1,212.92
August 29	11,286.58	11,539.25	2,510.99	2,562.11	1,177.91	1,210.08

Data reflect actual numbers of the respective indices; all dates are from 2011. For instance, on October 10, 2011, the Dow Jones Industrial Average opened (or began the day) at 11,104.64 and closed at the end of the day at 11,433.18. These data are not actual dollar amounts; rather, they are a number derived from formulae used to calculate each index. Each index is calculated separately, but in general they are averages (means) of many different stock prices.

Problem Statement

Trevor's Aunt Margret is a stockbroker in Sandy, UT. While he was visiting with her over Thanksgiving, he asked her some questions about the stock market. He has been interested in the stock market for some time and he is growing increasingly interested because he wants to invest some of his college money in an attempt to create more savings. Aunt Margret told him that the one thing most helpful for her while studying the stock market was to seek relationships between the market indices. By determining a relationship, she could make more logical investments in an attempt to increase her profits.

Aunt Margret decided to select some dates and data to send Trevor. After Trevor can prove to Aunt Margret that he has studied the markets sufficiently, she is going to help Trevor buy some stocks. Write a letter to Aunt Margret describing what, if any, connection exists for the three markets, given the data in the table.

Chapter 6

Covariation

The Health Problem

The Health Problem was written with the intent of encouraging students to explore a statistical concept called covariation. The word *covariation* may intimidate some instructors, but it is a concept with which most individuals are acquainted. It is important to deviate from the typical protocol of other chapters here and engage in a somewhat detailed statistical discussion, to create a distinction between covariation and correlation, given their striking similarities.

Covariation is closely connected to its cousin, co-relation (i.e., correlation). The two vary structurally in a very minimal manner because they each possess a similar purpose in helping statisticians understand how two sets of data relate to each other. With correlation and covariation, statisticians want to identify what happens to data set B when data set A has a certain appearance. With a correlation, one data set may increase while another decreases, or vice-versa, in which case a negative or inverse correlation exists. Alternatively, one data set may increase while another increases or one data set may decrease while another decreases, thus resulting in a positive correlation. With a correlation, the statistic (r) is reported as ranging from -1.0 to 1.0, or, if the correlation coefficient is squared (r^2), the value ranges from 0.0 to 1.0.

With correlation, one data set can predict the performance or appearance of another data set. Similarly, with covariation, one data set can also predict the performance or appearance of another data set. However, with covariation, statisticians are concerned with the amount of variance in one data set, or the amount that a data set fluctuates, relative to the amount of variance in a second data set. With the statistical procedure of correlation, the variance is not a pri-

DOI: 10.4324/9781003238201-7

mary concern. Moreover, with the covariation statistic, technically, there is not a limit to the range (i.e., it is not confined from -1.0 to 1.0 as the correlation coefficient r is). It is also true that, with covariation, statisticians are seeking patterns, similarities, and any generalizations or claims one might be able to make about the relationship between each data set. This is the point at which the two concepts appear to converge and differentiating between the two concepts becomes somewhat problematic. For the sake of students in grades 4–6, it is simply important for problem solvers to seek any relationship in the data sets and to try to identify whether or not the two covary, or seem to vary together.

The Health Problem is one with four data sets and problem solvers are asked to investigate a relationship between the first data set—the class mean for tooth-brushing efficiency—relative to the other three data sets, which relay information regarding amount of money saved, plaque on teeth, and overall hygiene. Each data set reflects data collected on students, and a class arithmetic mean was constructed to represent the *average* student in the class. Logic, coupled with a quick glance of the data, suggests that tooth-brushing data has a strong relationship with plaque build up. However, it is important to note the problem statement for this MEA. In the problem statement, problem solvers are charged with two objectives. First, they are asked to see "if any relationship exists between tooth brushing and the other data collected" and, true to form for a covariation problem, students are asked to look at the *spread* (a code word for variation) in the data sets. This last demand implicitly asks students to look at variance in the data.

Subject Focus of the Chapter

As stated before, the statistical focus of this chapter is on the process of covariation. Often highly trained statisticians find it difficult to competently explain the distinction between the processes of correlation and covariation, because the two processes appear very similar. Covariation differs from correlation in sophisticated statistical procedures and it varies, albeit slightly, from a conceptual perspective as well. Conceptually, the two processes vary because, with covariation, statisticians are concerned with the extent to which each data set varies. Nevertheless, each process is dedicated to the investigation of the relationship in the two data sets—hence the confusion between the two processes. Technically speaking, from a computational perspective, correlation coefficients can range from either -1.0 to 1.0 (for an r statistic) or from 0.0 to 1.0 (for an r^2 statistic). The process of covariation, on the other hand, can produce some abnormally large or small statistical values.

Links to NCTM Content Standards

The Health Problem may not attach to as many NCTM content standards as some of the others MEAs presented in this book. However, covariation is traditionally identified as a concept that is important to the development of young statisticians. Once again, it is critical to note that given the open-ended nature of MEAs, it is not likely that all students will solve the problem in precisely the same manner. In fact, when an entire class is divided into several groups and unknowingly solves the problem in precisely the same manner, it is typically an indication that the problem is too closed-ended, or that the teacher led students in one direction prior to solving the problem.

The following NCTM content standards have connections to The Health Problem:

- Find, use, and interpret measures of center and spread, including mean and interquartile range (grade band 6–8).
- Discuss and understand the correspondence between data sets and their graphical representations, especially histograms, stem-and-leaf plots, box plots, and scatterplots (grade band 6–8).
- Use observations about differences between two or more samples to make conjectures about the populations from which the samples were taken (grade band 6–8).
- Make conjectures about possible relationships between two characteristics of a sample on the basis of scatterplots of the data and approximate lines of fit (grade band 6–8).
- Identify trends in bivariate data and find functions that model the data or transform the data so they can be modeled (grade band 9–12).
- Use simulations to explore the variability of sample statistics from a known population and to construct sampling distributions (grade band 9–12).
- Understand how sample statistics reflect the values of population parameters and use sampling distributions as the basis for informal inference (grade band 9–12).

In addition, for all MEAs in this book, the algebra standard "Model and solve contextualized problems using various representations, such as graphs, tables, and equations" is met.

Questions to Pose to Students

It has been stated repeatedly throughout this book that having a strong set of questions prior to implementing the activity is paramount to success. Perhaps the most effective manner in which to derive a comprehensive set of questions is to solve the problem in as many ways as possible prior to implementation. In doing so, it is possible to see what questions are relevant to the problem. It is also important to recognize that not all questions will apply to all solution processes.

Some questions germane to The Health Problem include the following:

- In comparing the two data sets, did you consider that each range is not consistent with the other because all data sets represent different data?
- How did you track the relationship between the data sets (e.g., data sets W & X, W & Y, and W & Z)?
- Did any specific data set predict any other data sets better than the others? If so, why was this the case?
- How did you identify any relationships?
- Did you take a look at how close together the data were bunched or spread out in each set?
- Did you see any patterns that were consistent between data sets?
- Do any of your conclusions seem counterintuitive?
- Do either of these data sets seem to have a close relationship and similar variance? If so, why?

Potential Student Responses

Student responses to The Health Problem should be quite intriguing because the content matter and the foci of statistical procedures have become increasingly complex and developmentally more challenging from chapter to chapter. Consequently, to quote an old adage in the world of mathematics education: As concepts grow increasingly complex, fewer and fewer responses are precipitated.

Solution 1

Perhaps the most simplistic (and incomplete) solution is for problem solvers to create an arithmetic mean and to compare the data sets. From the arithmetic mean, problem solvers can see how far each piece of data deviates from the mean. Analysis of the deviation—not the standard deviation, specifically—is certainly one way to look at variability in the data (although it is not necessarily the most accurate way to do so). Problem solvers might also look at the spread of the data, and, if astute, they may also pay attention to the spread of the data to see how it looks in reference to the mean. In other words, problem solvers may help answer the question, "Is the data set spread out a good deal from the mean, or does it stick closely to the mean?" These two processes do not really provide a comprehensive look at covariation, but, if combined, they can help problem solvers realize that looking at deviations may provide a picture of how well one data set relates to another data set. Looking at the range of data in each set may also give some insight into covariation.

Solution 2

Another approach to analyzing the data is to compute all measures of central tendency (i.e., the arithmetic mean, median, and mode) and to then look at measure of spread by identifying the range in each set. This solution, like the previous one, is less efficient than actually finding the covariation statistic would be; students in grades 4–6, however, will not likely have been introduced to the computational procedure that would enable them to compute this. Nevertheless, the use of measures of central tendency and one quick look at the measure of spread can indicate the fact that problem solvers realize that the problem is multifaceted, as covariation is relative to correlation. After computing the measures of central tendency, problem solvers should seek the strongest link in data sets. It may be the fact that tooth-brushing efficiency links closely with plaque buildup, but it may not be the case that the variations are consistent from data set to data set. If another data set links closely with the first data set (i.e., tooth-brushing efficiency) and the variations are in harmony, then the problem solvers have an issue to resolve.

Solution 3

Perhaps a more systematic approach to solving The Health Problem is to look at individual data points for entire data sets. This process will be construed as somewhat cumbersome, but, if done well, it is a highly systematic process. Not surprisingly, the actual calculation to determine covariation is also quite a cumbersome process and, for this reason, this approach links relatively well with an actual covariation computation. Using this mathematical model, a group's data analysis might look something like the following table.

Analysis 1	Analysis 2	Analysis 3
$W_1 \ldots X_1$	$W_1 \ldots Y_1$	$W_1 \ldots Z_1$
$W_2 \ldots X_2$	$W_2 \ldots Y_2$	$W_2 \ldots Z_2$
$W_3 \ldots X_3$	$W_3 \ldots Y_3$	$W_3 \ldots Z_3$
$W_4 \ldots X_4$	$W_4 \ldots Y_4$	$W_4 \ldots Z_4$
$W_5 \ldots X_5$	$W_5 \ldots Y_5$	$W_5 \ldots Z_5$
$\ldots$	$\ldots$	$\ldots$
$W_{26} \ldots X_{26}$	$W_{26} \ldots Y_{26}$	$W_{26} \ldots Z_{26}$

In this table, W represents the number of tooth brushings missed per week, X represents the amount of money saved per week, Y represents the plaque build up, and Z represents the overall hygiene. The subscripts indicate the weeks (e.g., W_1 indicates Week 1), and the ellipses represent the relationship between the two data points.

The idea supporting this model is that problem solvers will analyze each individual data point relative to the corresponding data points in other sets. In so doing, problem solvers will realize the weak or strong relationship in each data point. The advantage to this model is that it can be highly precise. The negative component in this model is that, given myriad comparisons (78 to be exact), it could be easy to make a small computational error. Moreover, a system needs to be created to sum the differences (i.e., computing the deviation) and a control mechanism must be designed to accommodate the difference in range for each set. The easiest manner in which students could create a control mechanism would be to look at the data point (numerator) relative to the maximum value of the entire data set (denominator) and to then create a percentage for each data point. For example, the first column of the data table indicates that students missed seven tooth brushings in the first week. The maximum value in the data set is 11, so students could divide 7 by 11 and end up with .63, or 63%. By using percentages, students can accurately compare data across sets with disparate ranges.

In some cases, an inverse relationship may exist in data sets. For instance, it is desirable for plaque build up to be low, while simultaneously desirable for amount of money saved to be high. The facilitator should keep in mind that all data sets do not span the same range or represent precisely the same data, so a one-to-one comparison may prove problematic. As an example, the money saved per week does not equate perfectly with the amount of times one misses brushing teeth per week. A large number for money saved is desirable and a low number of tooth-brushing opportunities missed is desirable. Similarly, the amount of plaque build up on teeth varies from the number of times teeth are brushed per week, although the two are ostensibly closely intertwined in that the more tooth brushing is done per week, the less plaque will (theoretically) build up. (In this respect, it could be hypothesized that the two data sets might be closely intertwined.)

The real question with which problem solvers are left after implementing this solution is, "Does your approach account for the variation in each set, or does it merely enable the problem solver to identify a relationship such as a correlation?" This process helps problem solvers seek relationships while simultaneously enabling the opportunity to find possible covariation. As such, this model could be considered relatively strong compared to an actual covariation computation with software (i.e., something that is highly precise).

Solution 4

A slightly more systematic approach to identifying covariation—considering the fact that students are not expected to be familiar with how to compute covariation formally—is to look at the correlation coefficient and to analyze spread between sets. (It is suggested that the procedure for obtaining a correlation coefficient be introduced in the debriefing period following completion of The Stock Market Problem; for more information, see the Notes on Implementation section of Chapter 5.) In analyzing spread, problem solvers would look at the range and represent spread in some capacity, such as a scatterplot, to identify if any relationship exists in the two data sets (W & X, W & Y, and W & Z). In this respect, a formal covariation procedure is mimicked quite closely.

As stated earlier, the correlation process is a close relative of the covariation process. Hence, a good picture of how well the respective data sets covary will be provided. Secondarily, looking at the spreads of respective sets in relation to the other sets, although it will not truly provide the same analysis, will nonetheless help problem solvers realize what, if any, connection exists in the variance between the two sets. However a correlation is figured (even if it is simply approximated), the higher the correlation is, the stronger the connection between the two sets. The better the variance match in each set, the better the connection is.

Notes on Implementation

The Health Problem is a particularly difficult one to implement because it is perhaps the most difficult of all of the MEAs presented. As such, problem solvers should be provided with ample time to finalize their mathematical models. One of the reasons that the problem is challenging for young solvers not acquainted with covariation is because problem solvers are asked to seek a relationship and to analyze variation. Analyzing variation without a formula for doing so is very difficult, and hopefully students will remember this problem when they are presented with the actual formula in the future. Whether or not the procedure for analyzing covariation is discussed in the debriefing period following this MEA is at the instructor's discretion. Covariation is not an easy concept, even for high school and college students. Ideally, doing this problem will create a need to interpret and actively use a formula for covariation, hence increasing engagement in subsequent years. Based on the students' abilities, the postactivity discussion may be a good time for the instructor to formally discuss the statistical procedure for covariation, but this decision should be a local one. (If you are not familiar with it, the procedure is somewhat complex, and an explanation of the process lies beyond the scope of this book.)

Given the difficult task, a positive component of the data set is that the categories presented should not be foreign to students. Basically, all students have had some exposure to hygiene—specifically, tooth brushing—and saving money. They further may realize that failure to brush teeth will result in plaque build up, but the extent to which this happens may be difficult to predict because other factors, such as diet, can impact plaque build up as well. Hence, it is important that problem solvers create a mathematical model to be able to look at covariation with the data set.

Although it was not listed as one of the expectations (nor is it their responsibility to do so), problem solvers should nevertheless be able to develop three hypotheses about the data. These hypotheses can be made with respect to the relationship between data sets W & X, W & Y, and W & Z. That is to say, problem solvers should be able to speculate whether tooth brushing has anything to do with (a) the amount of money one saves, (b) the amount of plaque build up on teeth, and (c) overall hygiene. This data set and problem statement also illustrate the significance of creating a strong mathematical model because, in statistics, hypotheses are not enough to make conclusive statements about data. Although the data set is somewhat limited and small in scope, the data can help the problem solver see what, if any, relationship exists.

90   STATISTICS FOR KIDS

The Health Problem

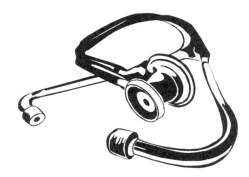

This week, the Bremen Health Fair will be held in the beautiful town of Bremen, IN. Residents have the opportunity to have several tests performed in an attempt to monitor their health status. For instance, citizens may have their blood pressure and pulse taken, reflexes tested, and blood tests and basic cancer screenings performed, among several additional tests. Often, senior citizens in Bremen participate in the health fair to learn if their health is satisfactory. However, the fact of the matter is that taking care of one's health is not merely a concern for the elderly. All individuals, regardless of age, should be concerned about the status of their health.

Along with her students, Mrs. Baker, a sixth-grade teacher at Bremen Elementary, is doing a unit on health care in which students are expected to look at their health by taking several measures. One of the measures that students have been asked to track is how regularly they brush their teeth. Each piece of tooth-brushing data recorded represents the number of times that students failed to brush their teeth after eating. Students have been asked to record several other measures as well. For example, students have been asked to monitor how often they failed to wash their hands before eating, how often they failed to wash their face before going to bed, and how often they failed to brush their hair before going to school. These data have been collapsed to represent overall hygiene.

Mrs. Baker asked students if they thought any additional habits were related to the condition of one's health. After a good bit of classroom discussion, students decided that they wanted to investigate whether or not saving money had anything to do with positive health habits. Hence, students were asked to record how much money they had saved each week and a classroom arithmetic mean was computed from the data by simply adding up the amount of money saved and dividing it by the number of students in the classroom.

After collecting some data and doing the analysis, students realized that they live pretty healthy lifestyles. Leading a healthy lifestyle is paramount to enjoying life. In addition to collecting the data and holding discussions on the analysis, students were reminded of how easy it is to lead a healthy lifestyle by eating a balanced diet, maintaining hygienic habits, getting adequate sleep, and getting daily exercise. The health unit performed by Mrs. Baker highlighted many of the desirable traits that students should seek and helped draw their attention to what they can do to maintain their healthy lifestyles.

Readiness Questions

1. What is happening this week in Bremen, IN?

2. What is one test that citizens of Bremen can have performed on them at the health fair?

3. What is one healthy thing that all individuals can do to have continued good health?

4. What data have been collapsed to represent overall hygiene in Mrs. Baker's health project?

5. Do you think there is a relationship between brushing teeth and overall hygiene? Why or why not?

Data Table: Tooth Brushing

	Tooth Brushings Missed Per Week	Money Saved	Plaque Build Up	Overall Hygiene
Week 1	7	8.21	6	5
Week 2	3	10	3	4
Week 3	6	5.75	6	6
Week 4	9	7.87	7	8
Week 5	2	12	1	2
Week 6	0	4.5	1	0
Week 7	5	1.40	4	3
Week 8	5	2.32	5	1
Week 9	8	7.5	6	4
Week 10	4	3.75	4	3
Week 11	2	1	2	2
Week 12	7	3.25	6	4
Week 13	10	15.33	8	8
Week 14	11	4.50	7	12
Week 15	3	10.66	1	1
Week 16	5	7.25	5	5
Week 17	4	8.25	4	5
Week 18	4	4.33	3	2
Week 19	6	9.00	3	3
Week 20	4	12.00	3	1
Week 21	8	6.33	6	4
Week 22	2	1.75	1	3
Week 23	5	2.87	4	6
Week 24	0	7.66	1	1
Week 25	0	10.33	0	0
Week 26	3	5.00	3	2

Tooth-brushing data were measured by counting the number of times that one misses brushing teeth. A missed tooth brushing occurs when one eats something and fails to brush teeth after eating. A high number indicates that the person has done a poor job of brushing teeth; a low number is desirable.

The amount of money saved is measured in dollars.

The amount of plaque on teeth was measured by counting the micrometers of plaque on teeth added from the past week. This was done by creating a mean after taking measurement in 16 different places in the mouth. A high number indicates that the person has a lot of plaque on his or her teeth. An instrument was sent home to detect measurements at this level of precision.

Overall hygiene was computed by taking measures on four factors and combining them to get one measure. The four measures are: how well one's hair is combed or brushed, how well one's teeth are brushed, how well one's face is washed, and how well one's hands are washed. A high number indicates that a person displays poor hygiene.

All data reflect arithmetic means from the class.

Problem Statement

Students in Mrs. Baker's class are interested in knowing if any relationship exists between tooth brushing and the other data collected. Specifically, they are interested in knowing if, when a change occurs in the tooth-brushing data, the other data react in some way. Mrs. Baker has asked students to investigate the spread of each data set to seek similarities.

Help Mrs. Baker understand what sort of answers she can expect from her students by creating a letter to her explaining your system for analyzing the data. In your letter, be sure to carefully explain how you performed your data analysis and alert her to how her students might analyze a similar, yet slightly different, set of data.

Chapter 7

Statistical Sampling
The Dachshund Problem

In this MEA, problem solvers are asked to look at a picture of data on dachshunds and estimate the number of each type of dachshund present in the data. In so doing, students are asked to identify to what extent each section of the data given is indicative of the entire population. This is a scaled-down sampling exercise, referred to as *statistical sampling*, which will ultimately help students understand the difference between a sample and a population.

Many activities and procedures in statistics have been completed with literally no consideration for the interplay or relationship between the sample and the population. By definition, the sample is the portion of the population extracted to be studied and ideally used to make a generalization about the population. It is imperative to identify a sample of the population that presumably closely mirrors and will therefore enable one to accurately learn about the population.

For example, if one wanted to investigate the thoughts of citizens on a new water treatment plant (i.e., whether or not a new one should be built), the best approach would be to study the entire population. The entire population would be all of the people in the city. But if, say, 100,000 people inhabit the city, it is not logical to think that all of the citizens could be contacted in 2–3 days (or any other short period of time, as is so often the case). As such, to accurately investigate the thoughts of the entire citizenry, a sample of some sort would have to be taken. Identifying a sample that is indicative or that will yield accurate measures of the citizens' thoughts is most important. To do this, several approaches can be utilized. An investigator, or statistician, could simply stand out in a park during a weekend celebration to seek responses. The

DOI: 10.4324/9781003238201-8

prospective problem with this approach is that the individuals responding to the items are only those in the park that day and there is no guarantee that they accurately represent the entire population of the city. In this respect, one could say that there is no guarantee that the sample is indicative of the population because it is what is referred to as a *convenience sample*. Alternatively, one could simply attend as many meetings as possible during a several week period (e.g., town council meetings, Kiwanis Club meetings, Lions Club meetings, Woman's Club meetings), but again, there is no indication that selected members accurately represent the thoughts of all individuals in the city.

There must be a more methodical approach that can be implemented to identify a highly representative sample. The best method is to use either true randomization or to use a stratified random sample. With true randomization, every single data point—in this example, every single citizen of our fictitious city—would have a perfectly equal chance of being selected for the sample. If 100 citizens were going to be selected or sampled for the study out of 100,000 total citizens, then each person would have an equally likely 1 in 1,000 chance of being selected. A true random sample is virtually impossible to attain when actual humans are involved.

A stratified random sample is another approach that can be used. It is highly systematic, but not typically as methodical in nature as true randomization. The reason that a stratified random sample (in short, a compromised version of a random sample) is not as good as a true random sample is because, to create a stratified random sample, one needs to have a representative number of individuals from each identified category. In theory, this approach is a terrific idea, but in reality, it is problematic to attain. For example, if the fictitious city were comprised of 53% African Americans, 28% European Americans, 10% Asian-Pacific Islanders, and 9% Other, then the selected sample of 100 individuals would need to be comprised of 53 African Americans, 28 European Americans, 10 Asian-Pacific Islanders, and 9 people from the Other group. The main issue with a stratified random sample is that, given the field of combinatorics, it is easy to identify a seemingly endless number of categories. This is due to subgroups of each category. Within the 53 African Americans, there are likely x percentage Democrats, y percentage Republicans, and z percentage Independents. Within these subgroups, a certain percentage of the Democrat African Americans probably like Thai food, while others prefer Italian food, still others prefer Mexican food, and so on. Some would contest therefore that it is virtually impossible to identify an accurate stratified random sample.

One caveat exists with sampling that is sometimes misunderstood in the field of statistics. Many feel that, if enough respondents are included, then true randomization can be assumed. This is a misconception. For example, if one wanted to investigate beliefs on issues related to the environment, it would not be fair to assume that sending a survey to 1,500, or 15,000, or even 150,000 members of an environmental association would yield truly random and impartial views on the subject. Thus, the idea that randomization can be achieved through sheer volume of participants should not be accepted. The sample used to represent the population needs to be closely investigated.

In this problem, students are not exactly asked to ascertain whether or not a sample is indicative of the population. Nevertheless, the background information provided on sampling should help when implementing the problem. Students will hopefully come to understand the pitfalls involved in sampling a population, and develop a strong methodical approach to overcoming this problem. Statistical sampling is an agreed-upon method that is used to expedite counting actual numbers in a population. In particular, this process is used when it is cost-prohibitive or for some reason virtually impossible to count the actual number of the population. For example, it has been discussed for use with the United States Census. Advocates of statistical sampling suggest that implementation of the process could save millions of dollars and, if done correctly, be just as accurate as attempting to count every individual.

Subject Focus of the Chapter

The focus of this chapter is statistical sampling (or as some statisticians refer to it, quota sampling—the more contemporary term, statistical sampling, will be used here). Statistical sampling is a process that most mathematicians understand, but they may not understand in sufficient detail. The Dachshund Problem has therefore been created to provide aspiring statisticians the opportunity to understand statistical sampling from a conceptual perspective. With statistical sampling, one analyzes a small set of data and simply applies, or extrapolates, the findings to a larger set of data. A common example would be to stand at the door of a newly opened pizza restaurant and count the number of customers by age range. From this initial small set of data, one could extrapolate and make inferences about future customer preferences.

Links to NCTM Content Standards

The Dachshund Problem is one that encourages students to consider samples and to further be able to generalize findings from samples to a larger population. In completing The Dachshund Problem, learners will engage in several NCTM content standards. For instance, learners are expected to be able to look at one section of the sample provided, not the entire sample, and make accurate estimates on the various types of dogs and then be able to extrapolate that data to a larger sample or even a population. In the process, students will become intimately acquainted with the difference between a sample and a population. The sample is always some portion, or a fraction, of the population. Moreover, students will start to contemplate the concept of *representativeness*, which is a consideration for how representative a sample is of a population.

The following NCTM content standards have connections to The Dachshund Problem:

- Formulate questions, design studies, and collect data about a characteristic shared by two populations, or different characteristics within one population (grade band 6–8).
- Use proportionality and a basic understanding of probability to make and test conjectures about the results of experiments and simulations (grade band 6–8).
- Know the characteristics of well-designed studies, including the role of randomization in surveys and experiments (grade band 9–12).
- Display and discuss bivariate data where at least one variable is categorical (grade band 9–12).
- Identify trends in bivariate data and find functions that model the data or transform the data so that they can be modeled (grade band 9–12).
- Understand how sample statistics reflect the values of population parameters and use sampling distributions as the basis for informal inference (grade band 9–12).
- Understand the concepts of sample space and probability distribution and construct sample spaces and distributions in simple cases (grade band 9–12).
- Compute and interpret the expected value of random variables in simple cases (grade band 9–12).

In addition, for all MEAs in this book, the algebra standard "Model and solve contextualized problems using various representations, such as graphs, tables, and equations" is met.

Questions to Pose to Students

This MEA is fascinating in that many individuals look at demands of statistics problems with little concern for how the sample was taken and/or whether or not the sample is at all representative of the larger population. Consequently, in this MEA problem solvers have been asked to contemplate an often overlooked, yet incredibly important, component of statistics. They should make the realization that great variation exists from sample to sample given the fact that in some cases data are bunched together and in other instances they are equally distributed.

Questions to be used during the implementation of this problem should be developed beforehand. Nevertheless, some questions will come up as students pose novel questions, and this is an impetus for solving the problem prior to implementing it. Some common questions might include the following:

- Would your mathematical model work in a similar sampling situation?
- Does anyone know what the term *statistical sampling* means?
- Would the model that you created be an efficient one with another set of data that may not appear the same as this set?
- Could you make a slight modification to create a more sophisticated model?
- How does your model compare with the other models?
- In your data, are all of the samples representative of the larger box? If not, how did you control for this problem?
- In what manner did you use your data to extrapolate to the larger sample?
- What is the relationship between your sample and the larger sample?

Potential Student Responses

Student responses from The Dachshund Problem provide a rich environment for a fruitful mathematical discussion. This task may not offer the varied number of solutions that some of the other tasks have; however, the underlying premise of realizing the interrelationship between a sample and the population is imperative to comprehending the most basic procedures and concepts in statistics. For more advanced statisticians, there may be one ostensible manner in which to solve this problem logically. However, one of the blessings of using authentically complex tasks with students of promise in mathematics (i.e., students who have not been educated in the field of statistics) is that they may generate highly creative responses to what appear to be relatively straightforward problems. It is important to reiterate that instructors should try to solve this and all problems themselves prior to reading potential solutions so that learning for understanding (Dewolf, Van Dooren, & Verschaffel, 2011; Heibert et al., 1997) can be precipitated.

Solution 1

A solution that some students choose to use in this problem is to count every single dog and to simply report the number of dogs. This is a less than sophisticated response and it really is not one in which a mathematical model is created. If this process is considered a mathematical model, it is certainly a most basic one. The objective in creating a convoluted box full of dogs was to scare problem solvers from actually counting all dogs. Moreover, the objective in doing the problem should be reiterated. The objective is to create a system or mathematical model that can be applied to a different set of data and be used with great efficiency and ease. Little to no generalizability exists in this solution, though, if done well, it does have the potential to yield the most accurate data of all solutions. But the issue of using this approach with a significantly larger sample (e.g., the United States Census) should pose particular problems for students who go this route.

Solution 2

A more sophisticated approach would be to carefully count the number of dogs every nth line and to apply that amount to the total number of lines. For example, students could count every four lines (thus collecting data for 11 lines total). With accurate information on one fourth of all lines, solvers can fairly accurately estimate the total number of dogs in each category. Moreover, the mathematics is fairly simple to execute and the issue of the law of small numbers may be avoided. With the law of small numbers, one must be careful not to predicate predictions and estimates on too few trials or too little data. In looking at every fourth line, solvers can proceed to a final estimation with a fair degree of confidence. Naturally, counting every other line (for a total of 22 lines) and therefore doubling the data sampled would provide an even safer approach.

Solution 3

Another approach to solving the problem is to use the grid system described earlier. With this approach, problem solvers create a grid that will cover the entire page. There are several approaches that may be used once the grid is created. A most natural one is to name each box in the grid and to randomly select (or choose) which boxes to count. Once the list of boxes is created, the grid is placed over the box of dogs and each type is counted. A systematic approach is to count some factor of the total number of boxes and to multiply by the requisite number to make a whole number (1/1, or 1). In the event problem solvers count a number that is not a factor of the total number of boxes (e.g., 10 out of 24 boxes), then the data can be simply multiplied by the necessary

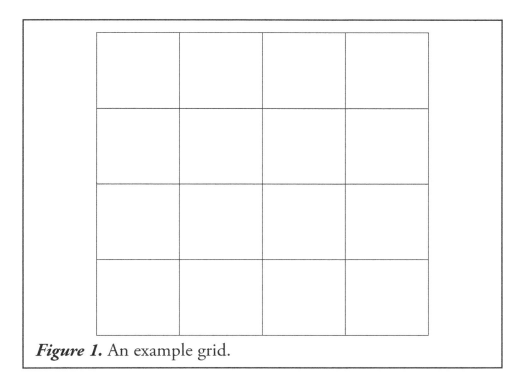

Figure 1. An example grid.

number. In the case of 10 out of 24 boxes, for example, all numerator data can simply be multiplied by a factor of 2.4 to attain the final estimate.

Two final notes should accompany the "grid model" solution. First, students may not necessarily create a formal grid like the one presented in Figure 1. However, as long as students divide the grid into equal areas, the process should theoretically work. Second, students will invariably be faced with the issue of what to do with dogs (or letters, as they appear in the table) that equally bisect two grids. Several options exist—for example, students could count the dog if any part of it appears in the grid, not count it if any part of it lies outside the grid, or create a different method altogether. It is important, however, that this situation be considered prior to proceeding with data collection, so as to avoid the problem of double counting. Double counting can occur if a dog (or letter) appears in two grids and is counted both times. The likelihood of this occurring is much higher if a system is not created beforehand to address this potential problem.

Solution 4

An approach that essentially accomplishes the same thing, and is mainly the same model (though some students might disagree), is to cut out the entire box and then to create a grid on the back of the sheet. From the back of the sheet, lines can be drawn (in the form of a grid) that are carefully made so that all boxes share equal space. Without looking at the front of the paper, the boxes can then be carefully cut and randomized. The interesting change in this approach, relative to the approach in Solution 3, is that, once the pieces are randomized, the data are very similar to a puzzle that has been disassembled. Problem solvers have no idea which piece originated in which place, but a sample of pieces can be extracted, the data can be counted, and the accumulated data can be looked at relative to the entire piece. That is to say that, if 40 pieces of the puzzle exist, then a certain number (such as 10) can be counted and multiplied by a factor of 4 to attain a relatively accurate estimation of the entire box.

Notes on Implementation

To reiterate, the best way for students to approach this MEA is to use something systematic, such as a grid (see Figure 1), to put on top of the sample. In this way, individual boxes in the grid may be counted in no particular order, in an attempt to make generalizations regarding the entire sample. When using a grid, it is hoped that students will learn that not all individual boxes need to be counted, contingent upon the fact that the boxes, somewhat randomly identified, are fairly representative of the entire sample space.

One concern that may develop while executing this problem is the question of what to do with highly unrepresentative boxes in the grid. This poses a problem in that it could easily skew data. A related issue that typically arises is the notion of what constitutes an acceptable answer, or range of error. And students may question how many boxes need to be surveyed (or counted) to carefully represent the entire large box (i.e., the sample space). This concept ultimately precipitates the mathematical concepts of the law of large numbers and the law of small numbers. Teachers may want to discuss these concepts with students during the debriefing period, but note that an explanation of these concepts lies outside the focus of this book.

When solving the problem, students should look for a pattern in the data to see if one exists. This approach will not prove fruitful, however, as no explicit pattern of data was entered in the sample space. Problem solvers should also invest some attention to identify whether or not the data appear to be grouped in one or more places. An example of grouped data may occur when several similar pieces of data appear to accumulate in one area. This occurred, to an extent, on the last line of data presented, in which an overabundance (12 of 22) of the letter *W* can be found. This might be because this dog, the full-size wire-haired dachshund, likes to be near other dogs of its type. Alternatively, it may be because one owner brought a litter of this type of dog. Whatever the reason, it is not likely that this data is representative of the entire data set, because full-size wire-haired dachshunds do not comprise 55% of the entire sample.

Some students may create a system that does not enable them to statistically sample the data set in a systematic manner. Therefore, the facilitator should have questions prepared to stimulate thought in case problem solvers create overly elementary solutions or they do not interpret the question for the full demands of the task. This can be done by illustrating some shortcomings in the solution. For example, some students will attempt to count every data point in the box. To counter this, the facilitator can pose questions such as, "To what degree of accuracy can you actually count all of the data points?" or "How is your system of counting all data points going to work with a data set that is 10, 100, or even 1,000 times larger than this one?" Often, flawed responses are easy to identify because problem solvers come to a solution prematurely.

The Dachshund Problem

Every year the American Kennel Club (AKC) compiles statistics on the most common types of dogs based on registration data. In the past decade, a pattern has surfaced and, in 2011, the most popular types of dogs, ranked first through 10th, were Labrador retrievers, German shepherds, beagles, golden retrievers, Yorkshire terriers, bulldogs, boxers, poodles, dachshunds, and rottweilers, respectively. Although each of these dogs is very popular, few owners may be as proud of their dogs as dachshund owners. This may be for several reasons: Dachshunds seem to have their own distinctive personalities, dachshunds are very energetic and brave, and dachshunds really seem to adopt their owners more than their owners adopt them. Among all dog breeds, dachshunds are notorious for being one of the most dedicated and loyal to their owners and, despite their diminutive appearance, they can be extremely ferocious and protective if provoked.

There are many ways to describe how dachshunds look. Some think of them in two ways: full-size and miniatures. Others consider the type of hair they have: long-haired, wire-haired, or smooth (also called short-haired). One can also consider the appearance or color of their hair. Depending on the expert, there are considered to be 5–10 different color patterns. Some of the most common are red, black and tan, brindle, sable, and piebald.

Known as "wiener dogs" because they resemble hot dogs, dachshunds were initially bred to hunt and capture badgers. This is the reason why they are long and short. Badgers are well known for being exceptionally tough animals, and the dachshund, which literally means "badger dog" in German, was the animal of choice for hunters, given its size, propensity to burrow in holes that are small and confined, and its ferocity as a hunter. Since their initial use, however, many dachshunds have simply become household pets, and they make terrific pets for kids, older couples, families, or anyone in need of companionship.

Readiness Questions

1. What was one of the top 10 most popular dog breeds of 2011, according to the American Kennel Club (2013)?

2. Why are dachshunds long in length and short in height?

3. What does the word "dachshund" mean in German?

4. What is one common personality trait of dachshunds?

5. Since dachshunds became popular, what is their main purpose today?

Data Table: Dachshund Hair-Length Distribution

```
Sss  W  Lll L   w w l   sSl LL ws      LS  WWW  l    ssw wlss  W L S S s ss l L wWWs Wwws lllw
w w s ss  W W W  SSLLlllss        S  LLlwls  slwwWw s   ll        LWWS  llWWsS   lswwwWsls
sslswlWwWsSll        SWWWLWLss    sllw wWlsS  LSLLwLL   SSsslwwW        ll        Ss
Ww    Llws  ssllwss  WslwWl  LLL  sSssS  WlW  WlSlslllsS  W            LllwsLwllss  Sssll  ssWl
WlSllw                Sss         WwwwlllwlslwWWl   SsLwlwwlslws                  ss
      W          WwwllwlsllwlsWLSLL          llwwSlwlslwW                  LWSLLwsllWlsWWlS
                WWLsllSWLLSlwwslwsllSL   Wl          WLsllswlswLLSlllSll      llSl
lSSll          LllssllwllWlssssssssslllwllLL     Sllwsllww      LSLLWWLSllslllwwwlsl
LSllwwls       ss      s      llw        SS      ss          llll      wlwlllwlls      lslw
      lsllwSlWW        WWLLsSSlwsllw        lslWsslw          SwwlsllwlSsswlssLwwlsllswllSWWSS
      WL            Lsllwlsllw       lSlwll  LSslwllLLLSWllWwwlls       l      lLL    Wlslwl
SLwllLLw       Slwls     LsllWWSSWWWWWWlSLL    LwssswLLw     LswWWllsWWWWWlsl  lsWW
SlSWllSwllwwllss     lwsl                WWWllswwllsslwlssllwllwsswls        llsLLL
WSSwwlls        lSllwll   LwwSllWllSllwlls     lsllwsWWlsSSSSSSWWSLLSSLLWWlL        Lsllw
SllW   SW           WWLlSllWSllwwllSlwllSwll          LwssswSlllSwwLLLLLLllllLLwSSllwsllSlwls
LwSllSlssl       LwsLLswll     Lwss           LwwsllSSllwSLLwwsLLWLlllSwwSllwSLwll
L                LwwlSllwwlsllsSSwSllwSLLWwllsLLLwwllsLwllsllwLSll                  lwl
                      LwllSllwslLSLSWLswlswSwllws WlllwsSwlwsLWlsWSwlws
LlsSLwwSLLWWslwSLlWwsSLWWWWWllSlwlSlwwSllwsl
Lw       LwwslSwlSlw  lwll    LlwslSllwsl    lLwslwllSllwsSSSSllwslSlwlwSLwslLwlsl      lSLlwS
SlwllSlwlslLwLwlSlwSlwSlllllllLLwSLLWWWllSll            LwslSLLWWllWllLSwlsSllw
LwSlwll            LwslwSLlwSLwl      LwL   lSwlL        LwslWl        LwslW
S          LwSllSlwllLLLSl
WlSlwSlwll     LWssLwslWlsLLLLwSWWSLwWWWWWWllSwwsSsss
LWsSllwslwsllwsllwSLLWWWWllSLLWLlSlwlwSLwWSwll
      wSlwwsSlwSSllWWSSWllWSLWSllSlwSLLwsllw        Lwsl        Ll        s
SllSllWLLSwllSllw


      LlwSllwlLLW  LlwSl          LWslWsl                LwSl  lwL   Llls
Slll             lwLwS lwsl        lswsllSwl          lws   lwslw        lls


Sllsl
LSLlw          Lws              slWwsllwsllWsllwsl      llwslwwsl          wllSlw
Sl             lSllwwwSLwL lwslswwl          lwslw          SssSlwll        slllsw
wLsllwSllw      Slw   Sllw       SlwwlWwl        llSlwwSl        SlwllW
Sll            Slwlls          SLws            ssslllwslWwllwsll      LswSw


S          SllwS        SwllSlwww        WWlLLsSSSSlLLWSwllSLw
               SLLSWS          SLLWWSlwWLL      SLwWWWl      SWWlSLLS
    SLLW        SLwwsllwslWWL  LLSWSWS  SW   S    Wl   LW   LW
    SSSLW
    SLLW        WLLS     SSL          LSLWWSL      WLSSWL
    LWSLLWS
        WWSL          LWSSLWS      LWWWWWSWWW                        s
```

l = Mini long-hair, *w* = Mini wire-hair, *s* = Mini short-hair
L = Full long-hair, *W* = Full wire-hair, *S* = Full short-hair

Problem Statement

Many dachshund clubs exist throughout the United States. One such club is the Nappanee Club of Dachshunds. On regular intervals, the club holds events to which dachshund owners can bring their dogs. Because they have no registration, the club relies on estimates of what types of dachshunds attend. This year they are seeking actual data to record. During their most recent meeting, they had a member get up on a nearby building to take a picture of the event. The picture revealed the data provided in the data table. For the sake of convenience, symbols have been used to represent dogs in the picture.

Try to use these data to help the club figure out an estimate of how many dachshunds of each type were present. Then write a letter to Amos Gibble, the director of the Nappanee Club of Dachshunds, describing the process that you used to estimate the number of each type of dog. Be aware that Mr. Gibble does not want you to simply count all of the individual dogs, because he would like to tally new totals at future events, and he does not want to have to count all of the dogs each time. Therefore, he needs a mathematical process.

Appendix A
Additional Information

The reading of any book is a journey. Hopefully this journey has been insightful and will facilitate true understanding of mathematics and statistics while simultaneously increasing affect (i.e., feelings, emotions, and dispositions) among aspiring mathematicians. In addition to increasing the affect of students, hopefully teachers, facilitators, and instructors have been inspired to try a new type of problem that was designed to genuinely challenge students of advanced intellect in mathematics in grades 4–6. After all, statistics activities and books are truly never written for this population, so this book was written specifically to serve this niche.

Using MEAs to Investigate Statistical Concepts

Initially, MEAs were referred to as *thought-revealing activities*. They subsequently came to be known as *case studies for kids*. The more formal name *model-eliciting activities* (MEAs) is the third iteration and perhaps is most indicative of their true potential. Nevertheless, the question still lingers: What is the actual purpose of MEAs?

Initially, the purpose of MEAs was simply to investigate how students think (Lesh et al., 2000). In short, MEAs were first created as a tool to research students' thinking. They continue to serve as an excellent tool in this respect because instructors are able to take a careful look at how students think while solving a problem. As a reminder, the processes that students use to solve problems and come to successful solutions are critical from an assessment perspective. Understanding how students think has rather vast implications on (a) selecting the next activity for students to do, (b) reteaching material, (c) making decisions as to whether to accelerate or enrich, and (d) manipulating affect (Chamberlin, 2002).

MEAs were later field-tested for use with teachers in professional development settings. A grant by Lucent Technologies enabled Dick Lesh at Purdue University the opportunity to substantially grow the number of MEAs in print and to field test the activities with in-service teachers. With this initiative, the ultimate objectives in using MEAs were to increase teacher content knowledge of mathematics, teacher knowledge of mathematical modeling, and the number of tools that teachers have to engage students in situations designed to truly facilitate mathematical understanding. Ultimately, accomplishing these objectives with teachers would increase content knowledge and knowledge of mathematical modeling with K–12 students.

The third use of MEAs was with gifted and talented students, and much of this took place at the Summer Residential Programs (SRP) at Purdue University. Students in several grades, predominately grades 3–8, had the opportunity to learn about mathematics and mathematical modeling by completing MEAs. Although MEAs were never specifically prepared with gifted students in mind, they seem to link well with their abilities. Further, because MEAs are sometimes considered an approach to acceleration and at other times considered an approach to enrichment, they have a tendency to be very useful in gifted classrooms.

Two final comments about MEAs are instrumental to realizing their purpose with gifted students. First, few approaches at the intersection of gifted education and mathematics education appear to be tested or researched like MEAs have been. Project M^3 and Project M^2 may be the exceptions to the rule in that they have been developed and somewhat heavily researched. MEAs enjoy a similarity to these curricular materials in that many empirical studies have been conducted using MEAs. Consequently, their value can be considered high in settings in which a research-based approach is demanded. One caveat, however, is that MEAs are not intended to serve as a stand-alone curriculum. Secondarily, MEAs involve students in precollege thinking (Lesh et al., 2000). This is significant in the respect that students are not often asked to engage in higher order thinking (HOT) tasks of this nature. It may be the case that many tasks intended to precipitate HOT among students come from somewhat trite situations. In short, many tasks may not have the realistic nature of MEAs.

Six Design Principles of MEAs

Briefly alluded to in the introduction, the six design principles demand that MEAs meet certain standards in order to be used as actual MEAs. The six design principles consist of the following:

- *The model construction principle*—Naturally, this principle stipulates that a model must be developed to solve the problem. Many terrific mathematical problems exist that do not demand that the problem solver create a mathematical model. However, all MEAs demand that problem solvers create a mathematical model for success in the task.

- *The reality principle*—This principle does not necessarily ask the question, "Could this really happen?" inasmuch as it asks the question, "Is this a school mathematics problem or a real-life mathematics problem?" It is hypothesized that problems that are more grounded in real life precipitate actual sense making (Hiebert et al., 1997) in mathematics. Logic dictates that this is true and anecdotal information substantiates this claim.

- *The self-assessment principle*—The self-assessment principle speaks of whether or not problem solvers can assess their products to see if they are within a legitimate window of acceptability. More specifically, problem solvers should be able to have an idea if the mathematical model produced will answer the problem accurately.

- *The construct documentation principle*—Unlike any other form of mathematics problem, when designing MEAs it is imperative that problem solvers are asked to reveal their thinking so that developers can investigate how students think. For this reason it is often stated that, with MEAs, "the process is the product." Hence, carefully documenting how the problem was solved is a requisite component of all MEAs.

- *The construct shareability and reusability principle*—With this principle, problem solvers must develop a mathematical model that has use in more than one situation. As such, developers of MEAs must create tasks that demand solvers to create mathematical models with some generalizability for use in future, similar situations.

- *The effective prototype principle*—This principle is closely tied to the construct shareability and reusability principle in that the model needs to be worthwhile (i.e., shareable and reusable) to be effective. However, another component of the effective prototype principle is that the model be as concise and simple as possible. Inordinately complex models are not typically considered as effective as concise models because of difficulties with interpretation.

All MEAs in this book meet the six design principles. Individuals implementing MEAs may choose to highlight various components of the problems pending their educational objectives.

Realistic Nature of MEAs and Group Products

The realistic nature of MEAs appears to result in at least three positive educational byproducts. First, the realistic nature of MEAs may be one of the explanations for why students of many ability levels can access and successfully solve these problems. MEAs have multiple entry points (Chamberlin, 2002), enabling students of various abilities to solve the problems. Moreover, some have suggested that MEAs possess the ability to help experts identify a broader range of capable students than traditional assessment measures can (J. Middleton, personal communication, October 21, 2011). The design features of MEAs may help students report high levels of affect (Chamberlin, 2002; Chamberlin & Powers, in press), which may further enable them to be engaged for longer periods of time, realize increased persistence, and ultimately increase achievement and enjoyment of mathematics. Others have speculated that MEAs have great potential for facilitating and identifying creativity (Coxbill, Chamberlin, & Weatherford, in press). This is because the problems are sufficiently open-ended and they all allow for more than one solution process. The open-ended nature of MEAs may help facilitate creativity in at least one of three areas of creativity: novelty/originality, fluency, and/or flexibility. Creating an impetus for administrators to use MEAs should therefore not be a difficult task despite the fact that MEAs may not match perfectly with the recent assessment of mathematics via state standardized tests.

The Impact of Affect in Mathematics

Affect is considered by many to be instrumental in the development of aspiring mathematicians. Much has been written about the close connection between affect and mathematics (e.g., Hart & Walker, 1993; Leder, Pehkonen, & Toerner, 2002; Mann, Carmody, & Chamberlin, 2013; McLeod, 1989, 1992, 1994; McLeod & Adams, 1989; Malmivuori, 2001) and the field of mathematics education is a content leader in affect and mathematics research. It could be argued that lack of agreement on a solid conception and definition of affect is an issue that has slowed effective research. That said, mathematics educators are in general agreement that affect plays a critical role in mathematics and the mathematical success of young mathematicians. Moreover, it may have strong implications for persistency in mathematics and the desire to take on higher level coursework. MEAs appear to have great potential for fostering positive affect in mathematics. Students generally report being interested in MEAs, and with this report comes many positive byproducts, given the close connection between the various areas of affect (Anderson & Bourke, 2000).

Relationship of Statistics and MEAs

It may seem to be the case to some MEA developers with an aptitude in statistics that these activities lend themselves to the creation of problems quite readily. In addition, statistics is a terrific venue for using MEAs because traditionally few grade 4–6 educators place an emphasis on statistics or statistical reasoning. Given the fact that statistics may be neglected in many grade 4–6 programs, it is important to engage students in thinking at a very high level and to simultaneously make the activities very accessible for students of advanced intellect. It may be hypothesized that the recent Common Core State Standards have reduced the emphasis on statistics in early grades. Therefore, presenting activities that enable problem solvers the opportunity to experiment with data on a higher level is an absolutely necessary ingredient to the upper elementary curriculum.

MEAs Are Authentic Problem-Solving Tasks

MEAs appear to be in a select fraternity regarding their classification as a mathematical task. In 2011, Chamberlin hypothesized that there were four types of tasks in mathematics. The four types of mathematical tasks are: exercises, word problems, problem-solving tasks, and authentic problem-solving tasks. Of the four types of tasks, the fourth kind, authentic problem solving-tasks, are probably rarest. This is because textbooks have historically and will continue to have a predominate focus on mathematical exercises. Word problems are prevalent in nearly all elementary and middle-grade mathematics textbooks as well. Legitimate problem-solving tasks appear less frequently, but can be found with some effort. Authentic problem-solving tasks are quite scant because they have a realistic context and ideally promote meaningful learning. MEAs fit this description strongly because they are serious mathematical problems that demand higher level thinking on behalf of the problem solver. Moreover, they contain authentic problem-solving scenarios for upper elementary students and they seem to match well with gifted students in upper elementary grades.

MEAs Precipitate Conceptual Understanding of Mathematics and Statistics

At the heart of MEAs is the notion that students cannot fake their way through the process. Either a robust mathematical model is created, or it is not. Solutions are attached to all MEAs presented so that teachers can have insight into what to expect for each MEA. Hiebert et al. (1997) spoke of *true mathematical understanding* and others refer to the process as *learning for understanding*. In either event, students must realize the actual mathematical demands of each task and create a mathematical model that explains the problem. For many, this is a foreign process, and analysis of data collected by Coxbill, Chamberlin, and Weatherford (in press) suggest that, as students do more MEAs, they become more adept at creating mathematical models. Familiarity with the creation of mathematical models is at least one factor in developing advanced mathematicians (Lesh et al, 2000). Consequently, teachers of intellectually and academically advanced students should think seriously about adding MEAs to their repertoire of teaching approaches in mathematics. In addition to providing insight into conceptual understanding, the cognitive demands associated with creating mathematical models to answer questions guarantee the completion of an MEA to be a significant accomplishment for students at this grade level.

Playing With Data Prior to Creating Mathematical Models

Playing with data prior to creating mathematical models is invaluable. It is not uncommon for statistics to be treated like so many other disciplines of mathematics in which students reduce the discipline to a series of memorized procedures. Further, the perception that many students may get from teachers of statistics is that it is simply a stimulus-response scenario; that, given a set of data, a certain procedure should be done, without thought. This is a disappointing manner in which to learn statistics. Ideally, aspiring statisticians should realize that, like carpentry, statistics is an endeavor in which several tools may be used to solve the problem. Some tools certainly work better than others, given the condition, and playing around with data can provide insight as to why certain tools (e.g., standard deviation or covariation) work better than others under certain circumstances. Furthermore, playing around with data prior to investigating formal statistical procedures provides insights into multiple perspectives. That is to say, when problem solvers debrief on various approaches to solving problems, flexibility in thinking may be promoted because solvers will likely come to realize that various ways to solve a problem exist and therefore an impetus to identify the most efficient way to solve the problem should be created.

Importance of Providing Ample Time for Data Manipulation

Playing around with data has an impact on learning formal statistical procedures. The topics presented in these MEAs are ones that will not likely be introduced for several years in the mathematics curriculum of these students. The main help that playing around with data provides is that it creates an impetus to learn the actual statistical procedures designed to solve these problems. In this way, problem solvers will not only realize an efficient manner in which to solve the problems, but they can realize that a high degree of accuracy can be attained and the problem will be accurately solved. To revisit the analogy earlier of the carpenter and a set of tools, the carpenter who uses a hammer to pound in a screw would ideally realize that it will likely work, but that a screwdriver would have been the preferential tool. Similarly, students who create less than perfect mathematical models to solve these problems will hopefully realize that their solutions are okay, but that there must be more time-efficient, accurate, and systematic approaches to attaining answers. Realizing the need for more formal procedures is one of the greatest byproducts that such problems can provide because it will theoretically increase motivation to learn statistical techniques that are more advanced than those used to solve these problems. Early research on numeracy (Carpenter, Fennema, & Franke, 1996) indicates that students require time to mess around in creating their own solutions to addition, subtraction, multiplication, and division problems. The researchers of the Cognitively Guided Instruction program further stated that students come to school with a great deal of intuitive knowledge about numbers and operations

(Carpenter et al., 1996). It could be hypothesized that statistics is consistent with number sense and operations in this respect. Playing around with data prior to learning formal statistical procedures may seem like a waste of time to some individuals, but it is an invaluable experience in developing true mathematical and statistical knowledge. It is therefore suggested that the approach presented is the most logical introduction to statistical procedures.

The Importance of Statistics in Everyday Life

True understanding of statistics is something few educated individuals ever attain. This may be a result of the aforementioned approach to passing statistics classes in secondary and tertiary schools. Sadly, it may be the case that even some instructors at the high school and college levels shy away from questions that might arise in doing these problems. Individuals who implement the MEAs presented must be brave because truly motivated students are likely to pose some very deep statistical questions. This is because these problems focus on conceptual understanding in statistics, not merely regurgitation of entry-level statistical procedures. In short, some profound questions that help students investigate *why* concepts work as they do will most likely be precipitated when doing these problems.

Couple this information with the notion that mathematics is considered by many to be a gateway to the full array of majors at universities, and ultimately vocations in life, and it is not difficult to see that true understanding of statistics is very valuable. It may sound clichéd, but true understanding of mathematics and success in mathematics is perhaps the major determinant in what major one pursues in college. An understanding of science, technology, engineering, and mathematics (STEM) does not indicate that one will necessarily pursue a STEM-related major, but having a poor understanding of STEM typically precludes one from pursuing a STEM-related discipline.

Additional MEA Resources

Perhaps the two most robust resources for MEAs are provided by Purdue University and the University of Minnesota. They can be accessed at the following websites.

- Purdue University—Case Studies for Kids! (https://engineering. purdue.edu/ENE/Research/SGMM/CASESTUDIESKIDSWEB/ case_studies_table.htm)

- University of Minnesota—MEA Library (http://www.modelsand modeling.net/MEA_Library.html)

The first resource, from Purdue University, contains a general list of MEAs. These MEAs range in the contexts and mathematical disciplines provided and they are not a database of statistics-specific MEAs. This is ideal for some, but not ideal for those wishing to follow-up on the concept of statistically oriented MEAs. No certain grade levels are attached to the MEAs at this website, but the range of grades 5–8 is considered ideal for their implementation with general population students. Hence, they are likely ideal for advanced mathematicians in grades 4–6.

The second resource, from the University of Minnesota, is one that is specific to undergraduate coursework and it appears to have a focus on engineering and statistics. The potential drawback to these MEAs is that, because they have been created for use with undergraduate students, their rigor may be beyond the intellectual or academic potential of students in grades 4–6. The activities may therefore require some modifications or at least a very serious commitment to solve the problems prior to implementation so that instructors are familiar with the difficulty of the problems. It is hoped that the problems presented exclusively in this book will add to the body of MEAs in publication and will aggressively challenge students in grades 4–6, as that was the intent in producing them.

Appendix B
The 10,000 Meters Problem, Solution 3

Dear Coach Hall,

As a result of our data analysis, we have decided that the following procedure should be used to offer scholarships to athletes. First, the number of scholarships available must be considered. If the coach has two scholarships to offer, then any two of the best athletes (i.e., the top five in high school, with a preference for any of the top three) could get scholarships. Alternatively, one whole scholarship could be given out and the remaining amount could be split between the remaining two to four athletes, again with a priority on the top three. If the coach has three scholarships, the top three athletes could be offered full scholarships, or one full scholarship could be offered to the top high school athlete and the other two could be split between the remaining top five athletes. Offering scholarships to athletes outside of the top five in high school performance does not appear to be worth the investment to the team or university.

It is important to note that the top five athletes in college usually come from the top five athletes in high school, although the order may not stay the same. By this we mean that the fastest athlete in high school is not always the fastest athlete in college, the second fastest in high school is not always the second fastest in college, and so on. Because of this, we feel it would be okay if the second or third fastest athlete was offered much of the money. Looking at the high school 10,000-meter data, we can see that the fastest collegiate athlete was the third fastest high school athlete, the second fastest collegiate athlete was the fifth fastest high school athlete, and the third fastest collegiate athlete was the fastest high school athlete. Similarly, the fourth fastest collegiate athlete was the second fastest high school athlete and the fifth fastest collegiate athlete at 10,000 meters was the fourth fastest high school athlete. The same pattern is true for the high school 5,000-meter data (shown in the second table), in that no athletes outside of the top five ended up being in the top five in college. The same athletes make up the top five in both the HS 5,000- and 10,000-meter PRs, but the HS 10,000-meter times are a slightly better indicator of college performance. You might want to keep this in mind when making your decision.

HS Rank	Name	HS 10,000-Meter PR	College Rank	Name	College 10,000-Meter PR	Rank Performance of Athlete: HS, College
1	Michael Kipkosgei	29:45	1	Mekonnen Demissie	28:51	1, 3
2	Keegan O'Malley	30:03	2	Assefe Bekele	28:58	2, 4
3	Mekonnen Demissie	30:04	3	Michael Kipkosgei	29:03	3, 1
4	William Kiprono	30:06	4	Keegan O'Malley	29:12	4, 5
5	Assefe Bekele	30:08	5	William Kiprono	29:27	5, 2
6	Moses Kigen	30:45	6	Moses Kigen	29:32	6, 6
7	Sean McLaughlin	31:53	7	Sean McLaughlin	29:38	7, 7
8	Dereje Tesfaye	31:54	8	Robert Ngugi	30:10	8, 12
9	Tim Williams	31:55	9	Martin Stoughlin	30:12	9, 11
10	Mel Stein	31:58	10	Mel Stein	30:36	10, 10
11	Robert Ngugi	32:00	11	Tim Williams	31:08	11, 8
12	Frank Lemit	32:10	12	Dereje Tesfaye	31:10	12, 14
13	Martin Stoughlin	32:12	13	Tom Brinkston	31:12	13, 9
14	Tom Brinkston	32:29	14	Brent Doerhoffer	31:17	14, 13
15	Eddie Billings	33:15	14	Frank Lemit	31:17	15, 16
15	Brent Doerhoffer	33:15	16	Eddie Billings	31:30	15, 14
17	Mark Berkshire	DNR	17	Mark Berkshire	31:38	17, 17

$$\Sigma = 28$$

HS Rank	Name	HS 5,000-Meter PR	College Rank	Name	College 10,000-Meter PR	Rank Performance of athlete; HS, College
1	Michael Kipkosgei	14:18	1	Mekonnen Demissie	28:51	1, 3
2	William Kiprono	14:32	2	Assefe Bekele	28:58	2, 5
2	Mekonnen Demissie	14:32	3	Michael Kipkosgei	29:03	2, 1
4	Assefe Bekele	14:47	4	Keegan O'Malley	29:12	4, 2
5	Keegan O'Malley	14:54	5	William Kiprono	29:27	5, 4
6	Moses Kigen	14:58	6	Moses Kigen	29:32	6, 6
7	Robert Ngugi	15:03	7	Sean McLaughlin	29:38	7, 8
8	Tim Williams	15:08	8	Robert Ngugi	30:10	8, 11
9	Sean McLaughlin	15:15	9	Martin Stoughlin	30:12	9, 7
10	Dereje Tesfaye	15:21	10	Mel Stein	30:36	10, 12
11	Mel Stein	15:28	11	Tim Williams	31:08	11, 10
12	Tom Brinkston	15:37	12	Dereje Tesfaye	31:10	12, 13
13	Frank Lemit	15:40	13	Tom Brinkston	31:12	13, 14
14	Martin Stoughlin	16:02	14	Brent Doerhoffer	31:17	14, 9
15	Eddie Billings	16:14	14	Frank Lemit	31:17	15, 16
16	Mark Berkshire	16:17	16	Eddie Billings	31:30	16, 17
17	Brent Doerhoffer	16:21	17	Mark Berkshire	31:38	17, 14

$\Sigma = 30$

The numbers in the right-hand column of these tables represent the rank of the athlete in the second column in both high school (Column 1) and college (Column 4) settings. For example, in the second table, Michael Kipkosgei had the fastest HS 5,000-meter time (Rank 1) and the third fastest college 10,000-meter time (29:03), so his rank is 1, 3. Similarly, Dereje Tesfaye had the 10th fastest HS 5,000-meter time and the 12th fastest college 10,000-meter time, so his rank is 10, 12. In using this approach, we can see how the first time can be used as a ranking for the second time. The closer the two rankings are, the better the predictor is. When evaluating the data, we paid close attention as to whether any of the predictors might help Coach Hall decide which athletes to recruit.

Commentary

The quality of the letter to the client in this example is very strong. Furthermore, the solution is sophisticated, assuming that the procedure for how to identify a trend was not provided prior to implementation of the MEA. The procedure is easy to interpret and it meshes well with the computations and representations above. The mathematical model used here would also help the students to understand the concept of correlation, which would be introduced later, in Chapter 5.

Finally, note that the sigma (Σ) represents the difference in ratings for all athletes combined. In the case of Michael Kipkosgei, his HS 5,000-meter PR was ranked first and his college 10,000-meter PR was ranked third, which makes for a difference (absolute value) of 2. When all other athletes' differences are summed, the total difference is indicated by the Σ, which comes to 28 for the first table and 30 for the second. The lower the value of Σ, the better it can be used as a predictor. Therefore, as might be expected, the HS 10,000-meter times serve as better predictors of college 10,000-meter performance than the HS 5,000-meter times do. Students should not, however, assume this from the onset. Because the students in this example checked both HS 5,000- and 10,000-meter times, the solution presented here is much stronger than it would be otherwise.

Glossary

Advanced intellect: The ability to think in a qualitatively more advanced manner than peers of the same chronological age.

Advanced Placement (AP): An assessment system whereby secondary students can earn credit toward college or university (tertiary) coursework.

Authentic mathematical problems: Mathematical problems with a context.

Bivariate data: A data set in which two variables exist that may be looked at relative to one another. As an example, one piece of the data set may be height and the other piece of the data set may be National Basketball Association (NBA) membership. A statistician could look at the relationship of variable A (height) relative to variable B (membership), variable B relative to variable A, and/or the bidirectional nature of the two variables.

Box plot: The box plot is comprised of the full range of numbers in the data set, and it represents each quartile (fourth) of the data when the data set is arranged sequentially from lowest to highest. The five number summary, displayed by the box plot, is comprised of the maximum value, minimum value, lower quartile (Q_1), median (Q_2) and highest quartile (Q_3). It is sometimes referred to as a box and whisker plot.

Case studies for kids: A name for activities that historically preceded model-eliciting activities (MEAs). They had all of the same design principles and structure. This term was used to describe MEA-like activities prior to 1990.

Common Core State Standards (CCSS): The Common Core State Standards is a document created by the National Governor's Association in coordination with the Council of Chief State School Officers. The document includes a section on mathematics and a section on English and language arts. Each section is intended to provide direction with respect to what concepts are central to student development in the respective discipline.

Conceptual learning: A type of learning that presumes that learners understand the theory (procedures) as well as the utility (application) of how the concept came to be.

Consumers of information: Problem solvers who have been placed in a situation in which they are required to think about previously assumed information that was memorized. For example, in The Taxicab Problem (Chapter 3), problem solvers are asked to consider the interplay between the (arithmetic) mean, the median, and the mode rather than simply computing the values. Further, problem solvers are asked to identify which to use given the data set.

Control mechanism: Relevant to this book, a control mechanism is something that enables statisticians to compare two disparate sets of data. An example of a control mechanism would be an F-Test.

Correlation: A statistical concept and procedure that indicates the strength of a relationship between two data sets.

Correlation coefficient: A number that ranges from -1.0 to +1.0 (r) or 0.0 to 1.0 (r^2). The coefficient helps statisticians interpret the relative strength of the correlation (i.e., weak, moderate, or strong).

Covariation: A statistical concept regarding the strength of relationship between two data sets. It also suggests that, as one data set varies, the other data set does as well. Covariation is considered a measure of the strength of the correlation.

Creativity: In mathematics, this term often refers to novelty (originality), fluency, and flexibility of mathematical solutions.

Data: Any piece of information, numerical or categorical, that can be used to conduct statistical analysis. It can refer to one or more pieces.

Debriefing process: The period after a (mathematical) problem has been solved in which student or group solutions are discussed orally.

Descriptive statistics (basic statistics): Numbers that enable one to describe phenomena (e.g., measures of spread or measures of center). Although they are simple to compute, they hold great power in rendering statistical decisions.

Equidistant: This term has two definitions. First, something or someone could be the same distance from two points. Alternatively, two things could be the same distance from one point. An example in statistics can be found by looking at the following series of numbers: 3, 6, and 9. The number 6 is equidistant from 3 and 9, and the numbers 3 and 9 are the equidistant from the number 6.

Flexibility: Regarding mathematical creativity, this term indicates one's ability to think from more than one perspective.

Fluency: Regarding mathematical creativity, this term indicates one's ability to create multiple responses or solutions to a mathematics problem.

Frequency count: The process of counting the occurrence of something. As an example, in statistics, given the data set (dog, cat, dog, fish, horse, cow, pig, dog), the frequency count of dogs is 3.

F-Test: A procedure used to compare the variances of two data sets. In particular, F-Tests are often used when the two data sets are markedly different from one another. This statistical procedure enables statisticians to control for differences in the data sets by normalizing the data sets.

Function: A relationship between inputs and outputs in which each input results in its own output. Two different inputs cannot share the same output.

Giftedness: A psychological construct that suggests an individual is advanced in one capacity or another (e.g., academically or intellectually).

Grid system: A system in which a grid is imposed on a picture of data so that a frequency count can be performed. As an example, the National Forest Service often uses the grid system to count trees after photographs have been taken of a plot of land.

Guidelines for Assessment and Instruction in Statistics Education (GAISE) Report: A document created by the American Statistical Association to provide direction regarding how statistics education should be conducted. A K–12 (primary and secondary) and a college level (tertiary) report were produced. The K–12 report was used to direct the writing of this book.

Harmony of data: The extent to which two data sets are similar.

Histogram: A graph that enables statisticians to look at the relative frequency of data (categorical or numerical). Histograms are often used to look at the distribution of data.

Instructor-moderated discussion: A discussion in which an instructor leads, but does not dominate, the discussion. The debriefing process used upon completion of MEAs is an example of an instructor-moderated discussion.

Interquartile range (IQR): The difference between the third and first quartile when data is sequentially arranged. As an example, given the data set (1, 2, 4, 5, 5, 5, 6, 7, 9, 9, 10, 10), the first quartile (Q_1) ends with the number 4, the second quartile (Q_2) ends with the third 5, the third quartile (Q_3) ends with the first 9, and the end of the data set is 10. The IQR would therefore be $Q_3 - Q_1$, or $9 - 4$, which is 5. An IQR might be used to look at the spread in a data set around the mean. Unlike the mean, and similar to the median, the IQR has particular applications in controlling for extreme values, such as outliers, in a data set. This is because, with median and IQR, outliers are just another data point, and they will not balloon or exacerbate the data set.

Inverse correlation (inverse relationship): This occurs when two data sets line up in direct opposition to one another, such as displayed below.

A	B
1	10
2	9
3	8
4	7
5	6
6	7
7	4
8	3
9	2
10	1

With an inverse correlation, the correlation coefficient (*r*) is -1.0.

Kurtosis: When looking at a set of data displayed graphically to see the distribution of data, this refers to the degree of the peak or flatness of the data.

Learning theory: The philosophy of how the information, material, or concept was acquired by learners.

Line of best fit: A process in which statisticians plot data on a Cartesian coordinate graph. Subsequently, a line is drawn that best approximates the data on each side of the line. An NCTM applet to help learners comprehend the line of best fit can be found at http://illuminations.nctm.org/ActivityDetail. aspx?id=146.

Mathematical modeling: The act of creating mathematical models to explain phenomena or concepts in mathematics.

Mean (arithmetic): A measure of central tendency and descriptive statistic computed by adding all of the data in a set and dividing the total by the number of entries. For example, the arithmetic mean of the data set (3, 4, 5, 8, 9, 10) is 39 (the sum of the data) divided by 6 (the number of entries), or 6.5. The symbol $\bar{x}$ is used to denote arithmetic means of sample and μ to denote arithmetic means of populations. It is important to note that a geometric mean can also be computed, although this concept is not addressed in this book.

Measures of central tendency: Sometimes referred to as *measures of center*, this refers to statistics used to determine average values of a data set. Such measures include (arithmetic) mean, median, and mode.

Measures of spread: Concepts such as variance, standard deviation, and range, used to determine the variedness of data in a data set.

Median: The middle number in a set of data when it is arranged sequentially. For example, with the data set (1, 3, 4, 5, 6, 6, 8), the median is the number 5 because there are three numbers (i.e., data points) on each side of this value. If the data set has an even number of data points, the median is computed by adding the middle two values and dividing by two. The median is considered particularly useful because it is not influenced by outliers, such as an arithmetic mean might be.

Metacognitive coach: A role adopted when trying to teach an individual or group a concept and using questions to guide the individual or group's thinking.

Mode: The most frequently occurring data point or number in a data set. For example, in the data set (3, 5, 5, 6, 7, 7, 7, 8, 9), the mode is 7 because it appears three times, more than any other number. It is possible to have more than one mode in a data set.

Model-eliciting activities (MEAs): Mathematical problem-solving activities in which problem solvers need to create a mathematical model to describe some phenomena involving number sense and operations, data analysis and probability, algebra, geometry, or measurement.

Moderate correlation: A term used to refer to the strength of a correlation, ascertained by looking at the correlation coefficient. Although statisticians are not in complete agreement on what constitutes a moderate correlation, a coefficient (r^2) of approximately .34 to .66 is usually considered moderate.

Multiple entry points: A term used in reference to mathematical problem-solving tasks that can successfully be solved in a variety of ways by individuals of various abilities.

Multiple iterations: The process in which problem solvers engage in creating numerous mathematical models in hopes of creating a better and more refined model each time.

National Council of Teachers of Mathematics (NCTM): The "public voice of mathematics education," this is an organization dedicated to promoting mathematics teaching and learning.

NCTM content standards: The five content standards are one of three sections of the Principles and Standards for School Mathematics (NCTM, 2000); they are comprised of number and operations, data analysis and probability, algebra, geometry, and measurement.

Novelty/originality: Regarding mathematical creativity, this term indicates the ability to come up with unique solutions to problems. Although these terms are not synonymous, they are often considered together as a single concept.

Open-ended: A term to describe mathematical problem-solving tasks that have multiple processes and (sometimes) multiple products.

Outlier: A data point that does not seem to fit with, or is abnormal relative to, other data. As an example, in the data set (2, 5, 3, 4, 5, 27, 3, 1, 6, 3, 5, 2), the data point 27 is an outlier because all of the other data points are single digit numbers. In fact, the number 27 is 4.5 times greater than the second-highest value in the data set. Several formulae exist for ascertaining whether a data point is technically an outlier. (For one possible method, see the Outliers section of Chapter 3.)

Parameter: A value that represents a population. For example, a mode would represent the most commonly occurring number in a population. Sometimes a parameter is referred to as a population parameter, but this term is somewhat redundant because the term *parameter* always refers to population, whereas the term *statistic* refers to a sample.

Percentage change: A piece of data that indicates the amount, reflected on a scale of 0–100, of change that occurred. The change can be positive or negative, and it is computed by finding the initial value, identifying the number change, and dividing the change by the initial value. For example, if an individual had 10 pieces of candy and acquired three more pieces, the number change would be $13-10$, which is 3. The 3 is then made to be the numerator in a fraction in which the initial number, 10, is the denominator. The percentage change in this problem would be 3/10 or 30%.

Population: In the field of statistics, this refers to the entire group that is being studied. As an example, if one wanted to know about the feelings of all members of a corporation and found a section of the corporation to study, then the section identified is the sample and the larger group (i.e., the corporation) is the population.

Principles and Standards for School Mathematics (PSSM): Mathematical principles (i.e., equity, technology, learning, teaching, curriculum, and assessment) and standards (i.e., algebra, data analysis and probability, geometry, measurement, number sense and operations, communication, connection, problem solving, reasoning and proof, and representation) determined by the NCTM to be relevant to K–12 mathematics.

Probability: The likelihood of an event occurring relative to the total number of outcomes. As an example, if four red marbles are in a translucent bag and the bag is filled with six additional marbles, the likelihood of selecting a red marble is 4/10 or 40%.

Problem solving (mathematical): The process of solving novel mathematical tasks.

Procedural learning: A type of learning that presumes that learners understand merely the procedure (or theory) used to successfully complete a mathematical problem.

Project M²: A curriculum designed to serve aspiring mathematicians in grades K–2 that are academically and intellectually advanced. Project M^2 was developed after Project M^3.

Project M³: A curriculum designed to serve aspiring mathematicians in grades 3–5 that are academically and intellectually advanced. Project M^3 was developed prior to Project M^2. M^3 stands for Mentoring Mathematical Minds.

Quartile: A subset created by dividing a data set into four parts so that each part represents one fourth of the entire data set. For example, in the data set (2, 2, 3, 4, 5, 5, 5, 6, 7, 8, 9, 11, 12, 12, 13, 15), Q_1 would consist of (2, 2, 3, 4), Q_2 would consist of (5, 5, 5, 6), Q_3 would consist of (7, 8, 9, 11), and Q_4 would consist of (12, 12, 13, 15).

r **value:** A statistic that represents the strength of a correlation (referred to as the correlation coefficient). It ranges from -1.0 to 1.0, with -1.0 indicating a perfect negative or inverse correlation and +1.0 being a perfect positive correlation. It is important to indicate whether a correlation coefficient is an *r* or r^2 value prior to reporting it so that readers can properly interpret which value you are referring to.

r^2 **value:** Also occasionally referred to as a correlation coefficient (see *r* value, above), this is simply the *r* value, squared. The purpose in squaring the *r* value is to make all correlation coefficient (r^2) values positive. When an *r* value is squared, the r^2 value will range from 0.0 to 1.0, with 0.0 indicating no meaningful correlation and 1.0 indicating a perfect positive or negative correlation. (Information about whether the correlation is positive or negative cannot be obtained from this value alone; to make this distinction, the *r* value must be considered.) r^2 values are considered weak (0.0 to .33), moderate (.34 to .66), or strong (.67 to 1.0), though it should be noted that these numbers are not always agreed upon by statisticians. Also note that, although their defining ranges may differ, the terms *weak*, *moderate*, and *strong* are used by all statisticians.

Random sample: A sample in which all members of the sample have an equal probability of being selected for the data collection process.

Rank order: A process whereby one looks at a set of data and arranges the numbers according to rank, from least to greatest (e.g., 1, 4, 5, 5, 6, 7, 9, 10).

Sample: The section of a population studied. For instance, if one wants to study the people of Indiana and selects a small number of individuals from some of the towns, then the group studied is the sample. The sample is more commonly studied than the population is, for various reasons.

Sample distribution: A term in which probabilities from a random sample of a population are described.

Scatterplot: A graph in which two sets of data are displayed relative to one another on a Cartesian coordinate system, in order to see if any relationship exists between the two sets. Many correlations can be identified through scatterplots such as the ones shown on the next page. Lines of best fit that are easily drawn often suggest that a strong correlation exists. For example, Graph A shows a very strong correlation, whereas Graph B shows a weak correlation.

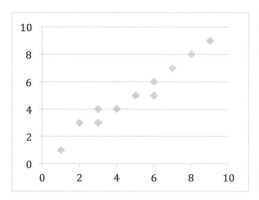

Graph A

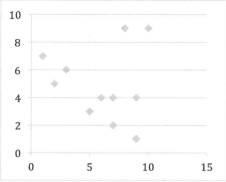

Graph B

Semi-interquartile range (semi-IQR): The interquartile range (IQR) divided by two. This statistic is less affected by extreme values than the IQR is, which makes it a good measure of spread for analyzing skewed distributions of data.

Shape (of data): The appearance of the data once it is graphed. Some data are mostly flat, some data have a lump (i.e., the mode) near the center, some have the mode near the right side of the graph (negatively skewed), and others have the mode near the left (positively skewed).

Six principles for developing MEAs: These are standards used to determine whether a written MEA can be called an MEA. The six principles consist of the following:

1. the model construction principle,
2. the reality principle,
3. the self-assessment principle,
4. the construct documentation principle,
5. the construct shareability and reusability principle, and
6. the effective prototype principle.

Skew: A concept used to describe the tail of data once graphed. For example, the graph shown below is negatively skewed because the data is largely nested on the right-hand side of the graph.

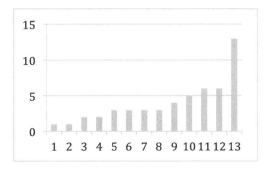

Spread of data: The total range of the data, from the smallest to the largest number in the data set. The word *dispersion* is often used in reference to spread. Instructors should note that this is not the only approach to displaying data.

Standard deviation: A measure of the variation or dispersion of data from the arithmetic mean. The standard deviation (sometimes referred to as SD) is often denoted by the lowercase sigma (σ), though use of this symbol has been omitted in this book. A low SD indicates that most data points have values close to the mean, whereas a high SD indicates that the data points are spread out over a larger range of values. For information on how to compute the standard deviation, see Chapter 3, Solution 7.

Statistical sampling: The process of looking at a section of data in an attempt to make generalizations about a population. For example, in The Dachshund Problem (Chapter 7), problem solvers are asked to look at data from a certain time to make generalizations about the entire Dachshund population of a small town.

Statistics: A field of study in which one looks at samples to make inferences about populations. In statistics, one may also study populations.

Stem-and-leaf plot: A means by which data can be arranged so that numbers that represent a set interval can be easily displayed. For instance, the following data set (23, 24, 26, 28, 29, 30, 30, 31, 33, 34, 37, 39, 43, 44, 46, 46, 47) could be displayed as a stem-and-leaf plot, as shown below.

Stem	Leaf
2	3, 4, 6, 8, 9
3	0, 0, 1, 3, 4, 7, 9
4	3, 4, 6, 6, 7

Stratified random sample: A sample in which each type of group is proportionally represented.

Strong correlation: A term used to refer to the strength of a correlation, ascertained by looking at the correlation coefficient. Although statisticians are not in complete agreement on what constitutes a strong correlation, a coefficient (r^2) of approximately .67 to 1.0 is usually considered strong.

Structural equations modeling (SEM): A statistical procedure designed to enable statisticians the ability to attribute or load factors to an outcome. For example, if a baseball coach feels that four factors are affecting a player's ability to hit the ball, SEM may enable the coach the opportunity to determine which factors are impacting the hitter in an order from greatest to least.

Sum of squares: The sum of the squared values of all numbers or data points in a set. As an example, if a statistician is working with the data points 3, 4, 6, and 8, the sum of squares would be $3^2 + 4^2 + 6^2 + 8^2$, which equals $9 + 16 + 36 + 64$ or 125.

Summary statistics: Statisticians do not always agree on the statistical concepts and terms that constitute summary statistics. However, it is commonly agreed upon that summary statistics include mean, median, mode, standard deviation, percentiles, interquartile range (IQR), minimum data point, maximum data point, and range.

Thought-revealing activities: A name for activities that historically preceded model-eliciting activities (MEAs). They had all of the same design principles and structure. This term was used to describe MEA-like activities prior to the late 1970s.

Trend: Any sort of historical pattern that exists in data. For example, it is often agreed that the major stock market indices are negative in the month of October because this pattern has emerged on almost a yearly basis. This can therefore be considered a trend.

Univariate data: A data set in which only one variable is represented. For example, data of a student's test scores (e.g., 87, 73, 94, 91, 82) would be considered univariate.

Variability: A term that refers to how spread or dispersed the numbers are in a set of data.

Variance: A term used to describe how far apart numbers are in a set of data. It is computed by finding the arithmetic mean and subtracting all of the numbers in the data set from the mean. All of the numbers that have been subtracted from the mean are then squared and added to find the variance.

Weak correlation: A term used to refer to the strength of a correlation, ascertained by looking at the correlation coefficient. Although statisticians are not in complete agreement on what constitutes a weak correlation, a coefficient (r^2) of approximately 0.0 to .33 is usually considered weak.

References

American Kennel Club. (2013). *AKC dog registration statistics.* Retrieved from http://www.akc.org/reg/dogreg_stats.cfm

American Statistical Association. (n.d.). *Guidelines for assessment and instruction in statistics education (GAISE) report.* Retrieved from http://www.amstat.org/education/gaise

Anderson, L. W., & Bourke, S. F. (2000). *Assessing affective characteristics in the schools.* Mahwah, NJ: Lawrence Erlbaum Associates.

Carpenter, T. P., Fennema, E., & Franke, M. L. (1996). Cognitively guided instruction: A knowledge base for reform in primary mathematics instruction. *Elementary School Journal, 97,* 3–20.

Chamberlin, S. A. (2002). Analysis of interest during and after model-eliciting activities: A comparison of gifted and general population students (Doctoral dissertation, Purdue University, 2002). *Dissertation Abstracts International, 64,* 2379.

Chamberlin, S. A. (2011). Mathematical problems that optimize learning for students of advanced intellect in grades K–6. *Journal of Advanced Academics, 22,* 52–77.

Chamberlin, S. A., & Moon, S. M. (2005). Model-eliciting activities: An introduction to gifted education. *Journal of Secondary Gifted Education, 17,* 37–47.

Chamberlin, S. A., & Powers, R. (in press). An instrument designed to assess affect with middle grade gifted students during mathematical problem solving. *Gifted Education International.*

Colliers International. (2012). *2012 parking rate survey.* Retrieved from http://www.colliers.com/en-US/US/~/media/Files/MarketResearch/UnitedStates/Colliers_2012_NA_Parking_Survey.ashx

Common Core State Standards Initiative. (2010). *The standards: Mathematics.* Retrieved from http://www.corestandards.org

Coxbill, E., Chamberlin, S. A., & Weatherford, J. (in press). Using model-eliciting activities as a tool to identify creatively gifted mathematics students. *Journal for the Education of the Gifted.*

Dark, M. J. (2003). A models and modeling perspective on skills for the high performance work place. In R. Lesh & H. M. Doerr (Eds.), *Beyond constructivism: A models and modeling perspective on mathematics teaching, learning, and problem solving* (pp. 279–296). Hillsdale, NJ: Lawrence Erlbaum Associates.

Dewolf, T., Van Dooren, W., & Verschaffel, L. (2011). Upper elementary school children's understanding and solution of a quantitative problem inside and outside the mathematics class. *Learning and Instruction, 21,* 770–780.

Garfield, J. B., & Ben-Zvi, D. (2008). *Developing students' statistical reasoning: Connecting research and teaching practice.* Dordrecht, Netherlands: Kluwer Academic.

Gross, M. U. M. (2000). Issues in the cognitive development of exceptionally and profoundly gifted individuals. In K. A. Heller, F. J. Mönks, R. J. Sternberg, & R. F. Subotnik (Eds.), *International handbook of giftedness and talent* (pp. 179–192). Kidlington, England: Elsevier Science Limited.

Hart, L. E., & Walker, J. (1993). The role of affect in teaching and learning mathematics. In D. T. Owens (Ed.), *Research ideas for the classroom: Middle grades mathematics* (pp. 22–38). New York, NY: Macmillan.

Hays, W. L. (1994). *Statistics.* Fort Worth, TX: Harcourt Brace College.

Hiebert, J., Carpenter, T. J., Fennema, E., Fuson, K. C., Wearne, D., Murray, H., . . . Human, P. (1997). *Making sense: Teaching and learning mathematics with understanding.* Portsmouth, NH: Heinemann.

Krutetski, V. A. (1976). *The psychology of mathematical abilities in schoolchildren* (J. Kilpatrick & I. Wirszup, Trans. & Eds.). Chicago, IL: University of Chicago Press.

Leder, G., Pehkonen, E., & Toerner, G. (2002). *Beliefs: A hidden variable in mathematics education?* Dordrecht, Netherlands: Kluwer.

Lesh, R., & Caylor, E. (2007). Modeling as application versus modeling as a way to create mathematics. *International Journal of Computers for Mathematical Learning, 12,* 173–194.

Lesh, R., Galbraith, P. L., Haines, C. R., & Hurford, A. (Eds.). (2009). *Modeling students' mathematical competencies.* New York, NY: Springer.

Lesh, R., Hoover, M., Hole, B., Kelly, A., & Post, T. (2000). Principles for developing thought-revealing activities for students and teachers. In A.

Kelly & R. Lesh (Eds.), *Handbook of research design in mathematics and science education* (pp. 591–646). Mahwah, NJ: Lawrence Erlbaum Associates.

Lesh, R., Young, R., & Fenewald, T. (2009). *Modeling in K–16 mathematics classrooms—and beyond.* In R. Lesh, P. L. Galbraith, C. R. Haines, & A. Hurford (Eds.), *Modeling students' mathematical competencies* (pp. 275–286). New York, NY: Springer.

Malmivuori, M.-L. (2001). *The dynamics of affect, cognition, and social environment in the regulation of personal learning processes: The case of mathematics.* (Unpublished doctoral dissertation, University of Helsinki, Finland). Retrieved from http://ethesis.helsinki.fi/julkaisut/kas/kasva/vk/malmivuori

Mann, E. L., Carmody, H. G., & Chamberlin, S. A. (2013). *Affect in mathematics: In search of an integrated model.* Manuscript submitted for publication.

McLeod, D. B. (1989). Beliefs, attitudes, and emotions: New views of affect in mathematics education. In D. B. McLeod & V. M. Adams (Eds.), *Affect and mathematical problem solving: A new perspective* (pp. 245–258). New York, NY: Springer.

McLeod, D. B. (1992). Research on affect in mathematics education: A reconceptualization. In D. A. Grouws (Ed.), *Handbook of research on mathematics teaching and learning* (pp. 575–596). New York, NY: Macmillan.

McLeod, D. B. (1994). Research on affect and mathematics learning in the JRME: 1970 to present. *Journal for Research in Mathematics Education, 25,* 637–647.

McLeod, D. B., & Adams, V. M. (Eds.). (1989). *Affect and mathematical problem solving: A new perspective.* New York, NY: Springer.

National Council of Teachers of Mathematics. (2000). *Principles and standards for school mathematics.* Reston, VA: Author.

Papinczak, T. (2010). An exploration of perceptions of tutor evaluation in problem-based learning tutorials. *Medical Education, 44,* 892–899.

Polya, G. (1945). *How to solve it.* Princeton, NJ: Princeton University Press.

Resnick, L. B., & Ford, W. W. (1981). *The psychology of mathematics for instruction.* Hillsdale, NJ: Lawrence Erlbaum Associates.

Stepien, W., Gallagher, S., & Workman, D. (1993). Problem-based learning for traditional interdisciplinary classrooms. *Journal for the Education of the Gifted, 16,* 338–357.

Weida, F. M. (1927). On various conceptions of correlation. *The Annals of Mathematics, Second Series, 29,* 276–312.

About the Author

Scott A. Chamberlin, Ph.D., is an associate professor in elementary and early childhood education at the University of Wyoming. His content area is mathematics education with a special interest in statistics. His research interests pertain to affect (i.e., feelings, emotions, and dispositions) and creativity during mathematical problem-solving episodes. Scott has a strong interest in mathematical modeling and feels that model-eliciting activities have particular utility with students of advanced intellectual and academic abilities. At the University of Wyoming, Scott teaches mathematics education courses to undergraduate and graduate students and he prepares preservice K–6 teachers to enter the elementary classroom. Scott earned his Ph.D. from Purdue University under the direction of Dr. Sidney Moon and his master's degree from the University of Utah under the direction of Dr. Don Kauchak.

Common Core State Standards Alignment

Grade	Common Core State Standards in Math
Grade 4	4.OA.A Use the four operations with whole numbers to solve problems.
	4.NBT.B Use place value understanding and properties of operations to perform multi-digit arithmetic.
	4.MD.B Represent and interpret data.
Grade 5	5.NBT.B Perform operations with multi-digit whole numbers and with decimals to hundredths.
	5.MD.B Represent and interpret data.
Grade 6	6.EE.A Apply and extend previous understandings of arithmetic to algebraic expressions.
	6.EE.B Reason about and solve one-variable equations and inequalities.
	6.SP.A Develop understanding of statistical variability.
	6.SP.B Summarize and describe distributions.
Grade 7	7.EE.B Solve real-life and mathematical problems using numerical and algebraic expressions and equations.
	7.SP.A Use random sampling to draw inferences about a population.
	7.SP.B Draw informal comparative inferences about two populations.
Grade 8	8.SP.A Investigate patterns of association in bivariate data.
High School	HSS-ID.A Summarize, represent, and interpret data on a single count or measurement variable.
	HSS-ID.A Summarize, represent, and interpret data on a single count or measurement variable.
	HSS-IC.A Understand and evaluate random processes underlying statistical experiments.
	HSS-IC.B Make inferences and justify conclusions from sample surveys, experiments, and observational studies.
Key—Mathematics: OA=Operations & Algebraic Thinking; NBT=Number & Operations in Base Ten; MD=Measurement & Data; EE=Equations & Expressions; SP=Statistics & Probability; ID=Interpreting Data; IC=Inferences & Conclusions	

For Product Safety Concerns and Information please contact our EU representative GPSR@taylorandfrancis.com Taylor & Francis Verlag GmbH, Kaufingerstraße 24, 80331 München, Germany

T - #0078 - 090625 - C0 - 280/210/9 - PB - 9781618210227 - Matt Lamination